THE SCHOLARSHIP GIRL

Life Writing

Abigail George

Mwanaka Media and Publishing Pvt Ltd,
Chitungwiza Zimbabwe
*
Creativity, Wisdom and Beauty

Publisher:

Mmap

Mwanaka Media and Publishing Pvt Ltd

24 Svosve Road, Zengeza 1

Chitungwiza Zimbabwe

mwanaka@yahoo.com

https//mwanakamediaandpublishing.weebly.com

Distributed in and outside N. America by African Books Collective

orders@africanbookscollective.com

www.africanbookscollective.com

ISBN: 978-1-77906-355-7

EAN: 9781779063557

DISCLAIMER

All views expressed in this publication are those of the author and do not necessarily reflect the views of *Mmap*.

Endorsements

As a society we rely on poets, writers, filmmakers and musicians to help us re-visit the past so that we can see the present in a new light and imagine what a better future might be. Of these creative beings there are some who are also brave enough to take us on their personal journey. Abigail George is one of these talented souls, prepared to bare hers by pouring out her life onto a blank canvas that she fills with wonderful poetic prose that places the reader at one moment in the cut and thrust of adulthood and the next in childlike innocence. This book is like a rambling river that streams along in tributaries of breath-taking poetic prose packed with forceful eloquence and an astonishing turn of phrase in a unique style that is at once fascinating and deeply challenging.

Abigail allows us onto her magical carpet that flies through her life like a random time machine glimpsing into the mind of a woman in all the various stages of her life and her process of self-discovery as she verges towards the glass precipice of suicidal depression and then to fantasies of love and romance with the hard edge of reality, loss and betrayal, and all the while with her hot monologue contrasting her self-doubt with her self-actualisation and her growing strength as a woman in a man's world.

Abigail grew up as a mixed-race girl during apartheid. Her family moved from Cape Town to Johannesburg to Swaziland to Port Elizabeth, where she now lives and writes. We learn from this, her first book, that it was poetry that freed her mind and at the same time it was poetry that reigned her in and that it was poetry finally that liberated her and allowed her to access her spirituality. Abigail's gift to the reader is a complex roller coaster that is rich and generous. This rare insight into a tortured mind is not an every-day read and I suspect that the intense images and thoughts that this book conjures, once it is completed and lying on your book shelf, will continue to resonate in your mind's eye and demand a re-reading and a re-interpretation as time goes by…

David Max Brown, (South Africa)
Filmmaker

This book is like nothing you've ever read: part personal memoir of a woman from Port Elizabeth, part praise song for all of literature's broken and brilliant souls, part potholed précis of South Africa's socio-political landscape, part prose poem which could easily be delivered in rap from start to finish, part complex family drama – and part love story (more than that: it is an investigation as to what love really should be). It often speaks of ghosts but always stays rooted in the fast-beating heart of the author. Reading it feels like dreams, and when you are done you are awake again, but different.

Toast Coetzer, (South Africa)

Abigail is the Eastern Cape's 'shining star' and South Africa's 'rising sun'. It is a commendable effort from a young and upcoming author. Congratulations and may God grant you a bright future.

Mr M. Jagernath (Dharam), (South Africa)
Retired educationalist and principal

The Scholarship Girl by Abigail George is a fine example of romantic fiction. This is a book on scholarship and experiences and the struggles to keep it alive. It takes us from personal notes to common phenomena of one's life where self-identity becomes more important. Presentation skills, diction and style used in the book give the readers an experience of enjoying some romantic poems; the elements of feminism, sensuousness, earthly pleasures and sometimes ethereal beauty attract the readers and make the book very interesting to read it from beginning to the end.

Dr. Vijay Kumar Roy, (India)
An Indian author, editor-in-chief of Ars Artium: An International Research Journal of English Studies and Culture (www.arsartium.org) & President of World Association of Authors and Researchers (www.waoar.org)

Table of Contents

Introduction

I have become weary of fighting wars. Of standing at the threshold of waiting. I have become wary of the experience that comes with the effort of sustaining love. I tell myself that I could never be with him because he was tall. Tall and beautiful. He had long fingers but all I could see was a balled-up fist. My head bouncing off a wall. Yes, he might have had beautiful hands. Spoke in educated and dulcet tones but I knew, in the end, he was not the one. K.R., R.M., M.B., D.B. were not meant for me, and in the end, came discipline, superfluity, human will, and the beauty of the small, helpless constellations found in strength. The seizing of progress, spiritual prosperity, and irony found in life. It is the strangest feeling in the world when the familiar, (youth), is no longer on your side. You're no longer the creator but a memory.

Once the memory was vivid. The memory of you had many colours. It, (youth), could sate your thirst. It had a depth to it, a dogged and serious nature, even an ego but now it has a false illusion that carries with it many secrets. A Namaqualand of flowers. A Namibia. The wasteland of an identity that could summon even flowers at will. The intellectual or physicality. To age sometimes feels as if you are making or rather moving mountains politely. With no wrong. With no wrong. Shaping valleys that sing with the force of winds, human beings, the sun, the bright shine of nature, the gentle genetic simplicity of the relationship between Noah and his animals. When it comes to the customs, the rituals of aging we begin to catch up to our parents.

Middle-age. Mortality, death, solitude and yet, we can still live. Fall in love repeatedly. Live in isolation. Laugh at will. In all of the profuse tidiness of mother-nature, the drama of leaves falling to the ground, I fill the hours with the pleasure of writing, interpreting the heritage that I find in water. The purity of the sea and the river flowing into that sea. Filling the ocean with the tumult of salt, light, life, fish, oppression. The wired wild fused with the voices, the waves, the cloth of both wilderness and wasteland. The autumn chill is impending and so is the solitary wave of the sealed letters of temporary discontent. These shadows of honey and milk. The action of the swarm that comes during the day beat with a rhythmic assurance. These shadows that have a self-aware awakening and with that comes the birth of giving. Grace. Mercy. Generosity. Memory. Yearning. Compulsion.

The birth of a writer's diary. Lines written after communion make allowance for a childlike imagination and for joy. Our lungs are furnished with guise, confidence, energy, matter. So are the distant genetic inheritance in our cells. The quiet found in our chromosomes. Our selfish organs possessed with the muscle of concentration. Focus. Clarity of thought. Speech silver. Silence golden. The silver linings of glory. The world is cold when you're a girl with no man by her side to teach her about life, or even a woman on her own for that matter, I have come to discover. This is written in praise of unity and solidarity amongst young men. There is a flux. Voids even in the origins of night and day if you look up and into the fabric of the eyes, the windows, the soul of the night sky. The worry of the touch of the dangerous and dejected despair of hardship.

I have the keys to the radiance of the ancient stars found in the realm of a dark city. Another rainy season, and I wondered what she's (my sister) told other people about me. After the silence, of winter rain that has moistened the ends of the world. Every branch is a living thing. Indigenous, familial or otherwise. Branches are full of meaning, silence, preludes. I'm so worn out with the energy of trying to live. Liberated and innocent she (my sister) walked the streets of Prague while I juggled my world in Africa meticulously. The sleep of my brother's child. The filament of nightfall in another country, in another Africa. The gravity of love after all these years, here is me letting go of rage. Letting go of solitude. Aging. Life. Grief and death. The milk and honey and manna of the fabric of difficulty. Sibling rivalry. The disillusion found in poverty. When I look into my sister's face and meet her eyes, it is like looking into another world. I have written this for the most part for her. Both of us coming up for air.

This world is still a world I recognise from childhood. It is like looking at the complex life of stars. A galaxy filled with constellations and starlit black holes. She's her own person now. You will find me writing, sitting at my father's desk most afternoons, or at my own desk in my room removing oppression from life. There are ways of diversity made of iron when it comes to gender. The opposite sex. The female gender. The song of the feminine. Children under the age of eight love my mother. They worship her. Fall asleep in her arms. They adore her glowing red lips. Her magazine hair and fashionable clothes. The scarf around her head to keep her hair in place. My father brought both a manic utopia and his bipolar life with him. The apocalypse. Wherever he went I followed. The dutiful little schoolgirl. I was always a little bit in awe of him. His high mountains. Complex rivers. The pastures in his environment found in valleys. I still am. Mum, well, today she's giving him the silent treatment. Thinks she has nothing to say to him. She's screaming at him at the top of her lungs. She called him a homosexual once but what's so especially bad about that except that he's her husband, and the father of her three children. She cannot bear to let him touch her anymore so they sleep in separate beds but in the same room. It's a bit like living on an island surrounded by applause. So, in return her children scream at her. Shut her out of their lives but at the same time, they cling to their mother's apron strings because she is all that they know of mother love.

Documentaries taught them about the assassinated writer and academic, Rick Turner, the assassinated communist leader, Chris Hani, that great leader, Patrice Lumumba, and the celebrated poet, Maya Angelou. If my mother had loved me, perhaps I would have been a different person. So, I write to silence the pain of the false illusion I have of her, and the inheritance she has given me. I write to cope, to feel a love, and a freedom. I write because writing is a form of therapy to me. It silences all the hurt, all the pain I've carried inside of me since I was an adolescent. So, I write through loss and chronic fatigue, unfathomable depression, watching homicide, crime, genocide, child rape, issues of faith while living on the fringes of society.

Please can I have some bread, cheese and red wine

I t began in childhood.

We were dragged to the library every Saturday morning, with our overdue books, and the outrageous fines we had to pay. Three children holding onto their library cards as if it was a golden ticket, a lottery ticket, a winning scratch card. Three children with bright eyes, gossamer hair, already with the most perfect volcano-garden inside their mind's eye, with the ladder of genes from an unconventional, cultured, educated daddy, an intelligent and elegant mother 'amidst-the-roots-of-oblivion', the looking glass of imagination, planting the stems of illumination, the feast of illusion, all the dimensions of possibility all found in children's books. The librarians' only 'communication' with us was with their phantom limbs when they stamped our books that we had to return in two weeks' time. And so, the three of us would depart with daddy. Walk out of the swinging doors to the waiting car in the parking lot. Our heads admiring 'our presents under the fake Christmas tree'. We would dance around our proud father.

Three children would look at the covers of their chosen afternoon, evening, future delight repeatedly deciding which to start reading first. Every book had their own silver lining, its own identity-kit of case studies, children who had complicated parents, and a humanity that was as complex as any child who kept a diary, a child's brain. The surface of the pages of library books, especially the Encyclopaedia Britannica had a certain down-to-earth smell like linen being ironed on the kitchen table, my old man, a pineapple, spaghetti, winter revisited as if it had had a wide exposure to the hands of many children. As soon as we got home we marched into our bedrooms as fast as our skinny-matchstick legs could carry us with the books as heavy as the weight of water under our arms with the love that we reserved for mummy, the awe that we had for our father, a school principal and the love that we stored up for Jesus (that's how much we loved reading. To us it was not just a hobby.) It opened doors. Gave us vertigo.

It was our cure in response to the childhood continued, our hallucinogenic medicine for Alice-in-wonderland. Her white rabbit and the fragmentary Cheshire cat's smile. We had a profound respect for literature, rigorous discipline and for silence. This had always been instilled in us since birth. Our 'feet stuck in a cement bucket' as soon as we began to read. We all read from an early age. In adolescence, it was Shakespeare's sonnets, reading newspapers in primary school and cutting out interesting articles that we would recite parrot fashion for our orals, and in the benches of the classrooms of high school English I discovered the "wuthering heights" of Athol Fugard's Mecca, Bessie Head, Lady Macbeth, Maru, and I discovered Salinger's Holden Caulfield sitting behind a school desk in Port Elizabeth, Swaziland and Johannesburg. Eventually we grew up. And 'it' (reading, browsing, instructions on writing, the Athol Fugard phenomenon, became our therapy; we were therapist-and-patient, psychologist and therapist's chair so-to-speak).

Writers became our waiting rooms. And sometimes the three of us could even see self-portraits of ourselves in the protagonists of the stories, which made us love the books, the respected writers even more. And then all five of us discovered poetry (Keats, Khalil Gibran, and Rumi). Hemingway (who needs absolutely no introduction), J.D. Salinger, J.M. Coetzee, Nadine Gordimer, Paulo Coelho, and Rainer Maria Rilke, and Sharon Olds. The North American paper tiger empress Sylvia Plath, the cuckoo-bird Anne Sexton, 'the black butterflies' of Ingrid Jonker, 'the anticipatory nostalgia' of Virginia Woolf, Jean Rhys, Anne Kavan, Ann Quin, Assia Wevill, Carol Ann Duffy and Ted Hughes. Female, feminist, protest poets, male poets, the war poets, the Romantics I fell in love with all of them. In the end, I could not make up my mind whether I wanted to be a poet or a short story writer, so now I am inspired to do both. The pressure sustains me in the climate of the hours and the loneliness of the primitive interloper.

When everything was still safe (in love nothing is safe, love regarded, love departed), sacred (childhood rituals are sacred) and there was no exposure to graphic pornography, substance abuse, domestic violence, letters to a brother in rehab, detectives in plainclothes in our house late at night (that would come later). I fell in love immediately with the colour of water when I was a child. A calm would settle over me. You could not take that calm away from me. All I would ever think about when boredom came over me in a classroom as I sat behind a school desk pretending to pay attention was her Sylvia Plath's lips, her mouth, and the deceased. The live wires of my dendrites existence would pale and I would forget that there were test tubes of my blood somewhere in a laboratory. I would swim lap after lap gracefully. The glass edges of my suicidal depression would dissolve into thin air, so would the colour of love, the lack of mother-love, my nerves aqua, my hot internal monologue would not be as hot as it was before.

Like rage, or perfume. For all of my childhood swimming pools were always inviting. Although I hated winter. I loved the cold.

3

Is it not strange, this stranglehold? That it has on me. Isn't it solitary? What does this beauty mean? Shadows and darkness come with this daughter. The splendid stars are not in isolation.

They coexist with the man on the moon. The decoding of the bloodline of lovely atoms and omnipotent particles. Those late bloomers. Photocopies of them. Her body remains untouched. The virgin suicide ballooning up into the ether. You are wrong. I love you very, very much. I love how you treat me like paper. I loved how you destroyed me. I loved how you sabotaged me repeatedly. I loved how you freed me, my chrysanthemum. My lotus flowering in the mud. I loved how you killed me in the end. That and how I stuck to the winter sun and needed no introduction to it. Out came gratitude. It had the energy of small hours of the morning, illness. And in the end, there was not anything of myself left. No more tenderness. I was not loved. I went cuckoo like a clock.

I was a serious philosopher, a deep thinker, screaming intellectual, a nun in contemplation, a yogi in meditation. A guru surrounded in an environment of marigolds with his disciples but my head's instinct taught me that it was not enough. Just the cold revisited. Another playground that felt that I was in the grip of something. Something grim. The jaws of something. Perhaps a bee season, or the harvesting of vegetables from the soil. Carrots, potatoes, radishes bursting with tap roots, vitality, ripe colours and health. I want to be a child again in my mother's house. I want to feel that splendiferous-anxiety I used to feel as a child when she pushed me away when I tried to make eye contact with her or just have a coffee. I wanted her to smile so badly. Instead in my thirties I turn to literature, to libraries, to feminism, to my writing grants, and you see I need to dream about the goals I had when I was a child and my

4

heart was full of gratitude for a father who sheltered me from a mother who did not love me.

And when I think of that elegant woman all I can think about is all the elegant and sophisticated women in the world and the long drives my father took me out on Sunday afternoons. He took me away from her. Away from the woman whose garden was filled with petals with a myriad of colours. Flying objects, leafy green trees, ivy. The sensual. The magnificent. The cold creature who I called 'mummy'. I wanted to tell the world I loved her but I could not. Her name was Catherine. It was not love. It was war. Of course, the bullets were not real only heart-shaped. Did I put that dark smile on her face? I would walk for hours just thinking. I never took my glasses off when I kissed her even when the night air was filled with stars and starlight. She was my wasabi, my sushi, my emergency service when I was out of sorts, out of balance. She helped get me through the day. She was tall. I remember that. I am a drunkard, a coward, as I close my eyes and try to forget those cowboy boots, those eyes, those eyes and I know in time I will forget. I will forget everything. And so, will you. And with it will come all these years and I have waited for nothing. Wasted years. Threads every single one. I am still a daughter though and that has not changed. My body has remained untouched for years, a knowing wasted youth, and a promiscuous youth. All I feel now is buoyant pain. And it hurts indescribably. I am twenty-two years old or perhaps I am younger. Perhaps I am nineteen years old on antidepressants fresh out of hospital. I am writing letters to the editor of my local newspaper to pass the time. I do not use a pseudonym. I use my real name. It is winter in Johannesburg and this is my first love affair with an older man. He understands me the way my father understands me. I say I'm terrified and he holds me close. I say, 'Don't leave me.' And he holds me closer still. Still I am afraid because I know how this will end. It will end terribly. I am no longer thin. I have convinced myself that men do not love women who have cellulite or stretch marks where they have carried a child in their womb. He takes my hand and tells me not to cry. Many women cannot have children. And he tells me that one day I will have a family of my own. Was this love? Was this it? And I look at him with tears in my eyes and I ask him, 'Is this as good as it gets?' Then we fight and he leaves me there in the hotel room with some money. And I cry myself to sleep twisting the sheets between my legs, clenching and unclenching my fists asking myself why did this have to happen to undeserving me? This was not supposed to happen. I was supposed to fall in love like my mother and my father. My mother got married at twenty-five. I am falling. I am afraid that no one will ever love me. I am afraid that one day I will be old and as I speak, I am growing older and with youth no longer on my side men will no longer desire me. It takes brutal guts to live in this world if you are without a companion, someone to go home to and the world seems a colder, stranger place than it has ever been before and you are the winter guest. You seem more estranged from people that you have not seen in years, been to school with. Your immediate family and you try to make connections repeatedly with them. Oh, how you try to make contact but their eyes are like ice when you meet them in person. The tone of their voices at the end of the line makes your blood run cold. And there you are just prolonging the intensity of the pain, the velocity and the density of the hope that you have that they will think you clever, find you marvellous, invite you to suppers where feasts are spread out on their dining room tables but soon you will find that this is no life for you. Moreover, you cannot fix this.

'Would you like to go to America?' he asks me one evening just out of the blue. 'You're clever. You can make something of yourself there you know. Study, work for an NGO, do research. What about an Ivy League university?' And he puts his fork down on his plate.

I never drink wine when we go out. I hate the taste of that stuff especially red wine and he smokes but I do not mind that that much. He is different when he drinks after a heavy meal. His lovemaking is different. All I want to do is talk about books, literature, documentary filmmakers and films. He thinks that I should go to the gym and work out. He thinks I am anti-social. If runners could slip into the fabric of time, then I wished I could do the same thing.

'I'll be lonely in America.' I say pouting.

'You're sulking now. Please do not spoil the mood of this evening. Be an adult. Be responsible for once in your life. Now you are not eating. Don't you like what I've ordered?'

People are turning around in their seats in the restaurant to look at us. They can probably overhear our conversation but I do not care if I am making a scene.

'It's raw fish.' And I pull a face.

'My baby doll. It is a delicacy Abigail and you always want me to be the one who orders for both of us. I asked if you wanted the roast beef and you said no. I asked if you wanted pasta and you said no. I asked if you wanted chicken and you said no. My heart really goes out to you. My heart bleeds for you. My heart cannot take the food you eat. Everything you eat is vegan or whole-wheat or pilchards or tuna or something that comes out of a can.' And as if he has said nothing, he continues to eat.

Girl, child, woman working in the community

The physical body is a strange thing. Blurred lines and all. It belongs to the parallel dimensions of another reality in mental illness, and in the measures of love. It is a wreck if you do not love its posture to death. 'What will become of me if I am not loved?' the physical body asks itself. The mirror becomes the looking glass. The reflection becomes a figment of the imagination when you can find nothing comforting in it. Yet the tortured poet finds beauty and elegance in everything. They take care to find something attractive in everything from birds, nature, and paradise to war. This is not by accident.

This is just a posture of a South African female poet and writer. When I think of alcoholism, sorrow and depression I think of Hemingway driving ambulances during the Second World War. When I think of paranoia, female depression, suffering, and bisexuality I think of Virginia Woolf and the affair she had with Vita Sackville West. When I think of Simone de Beauvoir, I think of the physical relationships she had with her students outside of the classroom. I do not think that sorrow ever leaves you especially if you experienced it in childhood. I believe it will manifest itself later on in adulthood but most importantly, as you grow older it borders on the ripening of adult flesh on the surface, while harvesting a tender feminine or masculine stem that will frightfully defy all logic. The more I read the more I come to the conclusion that the more we learn about the environment we find ourselves, the more we experience physically, viscerally, emotionally, mentally in the sexual landscape that surrounds us. We do not change. It is the minutia that we pass through that changes and must be investigated. We must turn inwards. Ghosts and starvation go hand-in-hand like the mysterious nature of sex and poetry and I say this because human love will not last a lifetime. Our appearance will change infinitely as time goes by. Husbands and children will not last a lifetime. But what does that have to do with the unquiet mind of the tortured poet? Everything. It is not the writer I want to talk about but the poet. Here I thought I would begin to talk about love in its most basic terms. The spiritual plane of it that levels all of us as we come into the world and pass onto eternity. The poet destroys reality but whether or not this leaves scars behind is not their problem. They want to be haunted. They want their poetry to haunt.

Here are some life events, people found in the unquiet imagination of a thinker, intellectual, philosopher, activist, that a female poet from Africa envisions. Reading poetry is a sensation that is fluid. It is nourishing this thin activity. It reminds of our survival. Our survival that is found in our blood, and the ladders of our genes. Survival is also found in the unquiet mind of the tortured poet. Death is just another location. To be oblivious to someone is like being in an alternate universe (paralysis). How do you communicate with this person, people that you love if you cannot embrace them, talk to them and it torments you. I think you give them a signal. When you are in love, it is almost like an illness, this stupor, this nameless disturbance. In addition, the poet writes, but what do other people do who aren't poets? They let life happen to them. They find that concentrated quiet word 'love' beneath them, complicated, and unnatural to them. The body of a woman is art. The body of a man is art. Art has both physical and spiritual dimensions to it like an empty mountain, the rural countryside, unbroken communication, old men and women reliving their childhood through flashbacks, memories and dreams and their own grandchildren.

9

There is alchemy in daily prayer when you release that element of the weariness of the world. Humanity when you witness the profound harm that human beings can cause to others, their folk, their tribe and their people. The female poet says, 'Beautiful boy, who are you (you meant an awful to me at one time and then we had a bad falling out)'. The canvas was propped up like trees. Here books taste like the sea, sea light falls through the pages, it tastes as if I am coming up for air, doing laps in a swimming pool princely blue. It has that image of waiting in the wings, the silhouette of forgiveness, and a portrait of the selfish, hungry me, that half-living thing I worship. With books there is the fastening of the mother tongue, an endless stream of consciousness fascination and catapulted wonder framework, memory work, the walking wounded, scars like stigmata, freedom of imagination in the method-actor is abandoning all rules of engagement on the stage. Books honour tradition. They say, 'Here is the heritage. Here is the exit route you have been following all of your life before anything wounds you any further.' Do men also have to struggle with equality; is there a nausea to solidarity? The apparitions in the poet's unquiet mind struggles with identifying romantic illusion and the glare of the appearance of the emotional.

Putting on my 'information science' hat: I love Hemingway. What writer out there doesn't? What tortured poet doesn't? I have been fascinated with his life and his women, his circle of friends, Hemingway "In love and war" and that he used to be a journalist. I do like American writers but not as much as like books written by people who write about themselves. My favourite book that I go to all the time is 'A Moveable Feast'. I ration it. It is a short book so I know it is not going to take me a long time to read it. I know what it meant to be homesick, hungry, a poor, starving artist whose only known survival kit was 'family' because I've lived my whole twenties like that. Hemingway, with his close-knit circle of friends and his wife who had a baby on the way. He would sit in a French cafe, eat onion soup with big chunks of bread, drink coffee, and think and think, watch the world go by, observe everything around him. His life was simple. He was a very complex, complicated man and so were his stories. He lived it. He wrote it. Some of his stories were exquisite masterpieces that were very simply written and so he became a legend. His writing was a brightening force in the world. (Why do so many writers like drinking coffee? I love drinking coffee because in between those gulps there are interludes filled with phenomena that make me think.)

Let it just wither away: (Whom do you love, whose writing do you keep on going back too religiously? Do not think about copying them, their style is their style and they have their own technique. Copy them in secret. Take words out that stand out for you. Rainer Maria Rilke wrote about many imaginative things. He has inspired a lot of my newer work. I would never dream of copying him because he was truly a master at what he did but I have begun to look at a bigger picture and all the details that God is included in. Rainer, he never lectured on his opinion on religion or God but that is not something that I want to do. When people inspire you they want to hear 'the outspoken you', 'your voice'.) All my teachers and mentors have helped me along this far. All my English teachers especially. But you must if you can speak in other languages write in your mother tongue because we do not have enough mother tongue languages in our side of the world. In Africa.

There is only Moses in the Wilderness: So, all I see is young artists and they ask me how they can publish their work, how they can become better writers? It has nothing to do with becoming better at it. They are already there. You have to be committed to your craft.

11

You have to take vows. There is a sacred contract between a writer and a book. Some of us become so wounded in the process of rejection (we see it as abandonment) that we never go back to what we have been called to do in the first place. We forget we are poets and that being tormented and unseen at the same time is part of the seam of the process. We are writers. We are struggling iconoclasts. We are all part of the iconoclastic-family. We are futurists. We are sculptors. We are already there. We just needed the elegant mathematics to help us along. Sometimes we neglect 'the gift'. There is a kind of alchemy in your head when you begin to write. It has its own machinery, its own wheels and all it asks of us is this? Write anything. It might not be perfectly edited. Just do not censor yourself. You need grit. It is going to take you far wanderer like Moses in the wilderness. All compositions that are aligned for art's sake and in hardship, trial and despair, that desperation, sly in the voice and mind of the cuckoo living wasteland of the tortured poet is mine, mine for the taking. Breath-taking is just as important as impoverished courage might seem to be sometimes worth it. It is not just the festival of it that amuses me, pours itself into me, the physical me, it is all the elements. Greatness lies in the peace it gives me.

Read much. Read everything you can get your hands on because it will not just inspire you, it will inspire your imagination and your subconsciousness. Perhaps silence is the best answer, (guardian angels have swords and humanity has silence). Do not spend all your time thinking of all the negativity in the world. Laugh. Smile. Become aware of just how much you have to be grateful for, for every lesson is a breathing lesson, a celestial navigation on this patchwork planet (my entire favourite reads by Anne Tyler).

Just think of what came before is now gone. Past is past, intellectual thinkers, ego, psyche, that psychological framework. Well now, there is only personal space, future living and soul retrieval, consciousness travelling across the globe. What I believed to be before, as truth has become knowledge. And isn't knowledge powerful? Knowledge of the present situations taking place all over the world mostly conflict, mostly war, mostly brutality from man against man and vulnerable women and children caught in the middle.

Coming home from the sea

I remember great poets, and I recognise that I am getting older, more set in my ways, moving forward towards something impenetrable, invincible and that I'm protected in this mysterious world, projecting myself forward into a future not filled with spiritual poverty, or wealth that is known as prosperity and being grounded by the gravity of Mother Earth, joy (Beethoven, Tchaikovsky), the Russian writers (Nabokov's Lolita which wounded me, and that taught me that we learn from our scars, we are not our scars, we are not our wounds, it is just part of our personal journey, our psyche, the teeth sunken into my personality), and Kubrick. So Abigail George has become A. George.

Failure can hurt. Young girls who think they will be goddesses forever can hurt you just like publishers with their neatly typed (by their secretaries who wear their hair in chignons) rejection letters (forgive them for they know not what they do), other writers who have won more prizes than you have, who have the world eating out of their hands (forgive them for they know not what they do)? Do you understand that? Do you understand compulsion? Do you understand the complexities now in the mind of the poet and that there is an unstoppable fine line, a psychological thread that borders the finesse of the writer and the instinct of the poet? Then there are films, which are at the very fabric of our human nature. They are like a flame. They reverberate with a kind of poignancy. Meanwhile poetry is like an invisible woman while films are the art form of this century and I have to confess that I miss it, I miss the medium. So the poets come, the greats come and they guide me on this journey, this route like Saints when they come marching through my

14

consciousness like child soldiers. It's unnatural, disturbing, an avalanche of them, an avalanche of thoughts of Anna Kavan's ice or asylum piece. There's no light only night (the night of an insomniac). And if I have to examine the unquiet mind of the poet I would say that it is included in all of that I have mentioned above.

Despair is painful when it comes to rewriting drafts of poetry and it is easy to feel disillusioned. It is easy to become a Buddhist monk in a second but keep at it. Do not retreat. It is easy to become distracted by other people's insults but still you must keep at it. Because believe you me you will reach a stage where what you are writing as a poet, that is which is hardwired to your brain, that which is authentic, will suddenly become brilliant on the page and someone will take knowledge away with them from something that you thought was nothingness. It is powerful to be honest. There are not a lot of honest people left in this world. Then possibilities will be endless. One person will become two and so forth and so forth.

Sometimes I do not understand life but I know I must make sense of the pride that people have, the racism that they keep close to their hearts, their egos, their narcissistic identities, their flesh and blood. Humanity needs these personal experiences to become more and more elevated, as they move closer and closer to their true home which is to recover their harmonic spirit, release the woundedness of the past and accept that the physical body is just that, a vessel and sometimes an empty one at that because we are living with so many material possessions around us, beautiful and valuable things in 'many rooms of mansions'. Perhaps that is why so many of us feel loneliness, despair, hardship, suffering and we sometimes feel that we deserve an award for the role that we play in this world-drama.

Therefore, we come to the summing up, the words of shamanic wisdom.

I believe in gratitude, abundance, blessings, and angels above on the astral-plane and on the earth-plane, foundations, goals and dreams.

Because without dreaming, without writing poetry, without the unseen and tortured consciousness we would have no dreams, no visionaries, no awareness, only introverted leaders, the internal struggle within all of us that either instructs us in a pure direction or corrects us to go to a higher level, connects us with others. Humanity is made up of love, some of it is unconditional, some parts of it is inherited, and love is not just a ritual, a relic, or an ornament. How else do you explain how far we have come, our journeys, and our paths that have coincided with historical events that have changed the course of humanity?

Winter is the perfect time to rest. There is a lightness and a being in the air. Now there is only time for 'botanical drawings of observations', a palace, the throne room, metaphors, and for growing older, the illustration of a dark horse of a man growing dimmer and dimmer. Childhood transformations have come, gone taking bedtime stories, Disney, and chipped teeth with them. Family history, imagination, the wilderness. When the world feels apocalyptic. When your mind's eye sits through silences. The day your parents told you they were both going to separate or divorce and you felt like an interloper. I was the chosen one in summer, spring, winter and autumn. The tortured poet says, 'I was the self-losing tree with its beautiful leaves. The abundance of moths betrayed by the light. I am the sonnet, the pleasurable food chain, the preparation of the sheltered golden roast in the oven, and I am a refuge from progress, regions of green feasts for the eyes. I am a swimmer in a public domain. Love is my life belt. It gives me self-preservation.' 'Poetry,' says the tortured poet, 'gives me a drowning helplessness, sustains me, and fuses my cheap pleasures that I get out of fashioning solitude. And when I entangle myself in the oppression of intimacy, and the proportions of misery that sometimes come with it I must carry on secretly with my life work in order for the feminine not to be altered but to be praised, worshiped confidently, to make her pure and significant and the fundamental masculine to be esteemed. Not distorted, displaced, or limited in any way by dark behaviour or a masked disguise.'

As much as it is begun to be said, Africa is a country. A continent marked by both brown, black, and white faces, the Malay culture, the European immigrants that have settled here, the Afrikaners', Chinese, the liberals, and those of mixed race descent. Africa is an energetic, depressed, traumatic continent where you can make abstract drawings of people just by observing them. And for those who like alien and hallucinatory prose I only have two words for you. Go back. Go back to gossip (what will you find there you might be asking yourself. You will find illuminating words.) Go back to poetry, talk to your children, your spouse, even the frailty of the elderly, the infirm, the noise of your young, boisterous family and there you will find the same thing. You cannot erase language because language crowds everything out. You cannot erase touch because touch crowds everything out. You cannot erase the unseen, the unquiet mind of the tortured poet because it drowns everything out.

Something is beginning to shift inside me. Therefore, I must begin to speak to the one that I love, about the one that I love, the unseen, the unquiet, and the tortured. I am often left with this question of where my home is. I know where my battlefields are and my playing grounds but where is home. My home is where the sea meets the shore's feast and the river's mouth. It is in my lap and arms in my hands like black water or blackstrap molasses. I am poured into Hollywood's grave where the shallows swim into J. D. Salinger (into you). The roses are lovely this time of year. Everest is listening. Pound's second Alba. You are no stranger to legend. When I look at you, any photograph of you, it is as if some power switch has gone off inside of me. Parachutes fall from the skies and a wilderness history rises up out of darkness and history. What I will remember of you is this? The elixir of the waves of your dark hair. You tiger. All the details of you. Your rough magic trivia. Once upon a time, you were my poetry, Salinger. (Can torment be poetry in and of itself? I think so). I walked tall and pretty my high and pale September friend. Once I followed the bittersweet blueprint of angels but now I feel like yellow sunlight and a field of stars dead to the imagination. Of other poets and I am left missing you (again I speak of the torment of the poet here. The torment, which is unspecified and indefinable). Anguish fills my heart. Words do as paper dolls do. They are nothing but pretence. There is no substance to a paper doll. What can curb its dangerously mysterious anxiousness, its depression that it develops into, and what can it exchange for the solidity and substance, hours of contradictions of life. How can it grasp anything of life, the simplicity, the sadness, duplicity and the happiness of childhood?

Pain has a muscle multiplied. An adolescent's moodiness, defensiveness, and the hours for them only consists of a schizophrenic harmony whether they are sad, or happy, or pensive, or have a longing rising up with them and it is only a poet with their unquiet mind who can understand the depths of the isolation and rejection that sometimes this young adult feels on the periphery of an

18

adult world that he or she does not yet fully comprehend or can understand.

And there found in the translation of pain (of physical torment and the pain of the mind) love is a ghost with serious intent. It is heavy illumined with light and salt. Heavy with your laughter and it is a wonderland of people. It is a wonderland of traffic.

Who is the 'you' I am speaking to or rather referring to here? Is it not the unquiet mind of the poet?

The sun and days compensate for the lack of you. Now we talk about love/poetry as if it is a mountain. We want to hike to the stars and forget about our hearts and what startled us into believing that we cannot live forever. 'Love is not love when it alteration finds.' Shakespeare said that with a genuine and artistic sensibility.

I believe in God now. This is what I know for sure. When I was in my teens, He was irrelevant. Then one day I got sick-sick. The illness (lithium toxicity) that had come silently out of nowhere (because I hadn't been having regular blood tests) had made me slip into a coma for two weeks; then out of the blue I woke up one morning in the hospital. I could not speak but I could see. I could not walk. I was in a lot of pain. I was in ICU. I do not remember a lot of that time only that estranged family came to visit. I cannot recollect conversations only that people who were never there for me before suddenly appeared at my bedside and they prayed for me. Well, years have passed, and even though I was hurt in church now I believe in God and that He instructs my writing, my befuddled passion as I gather all the accumulations of my lifetime so far. He has to be found in the reliable source of the generous details and as I experiment with the machinery of words. It is becoming more and more naturally to me now. Writing I have learnt does not only come with a spiralling intuition; it also comes with a unique spiritual awareness.

Unlikely stories.

This transition of the streaming of words; gifted fragments from my mind to the page makes me feel like an ancient fossil steeped, enriched with history. It leaves me drowning like the leaves spilling down a drain during a downpour. My writing promises a generation love and the calling of imagination; to journey gently on a river wide no matter what I was faced with; glass ceilings, brick walls, floods in reality and floods that were surreal, Dadaist, swirling in my head space, surfaces of pools that were both telling of rings and circles of my inherent moods and reflections, the inner spaces of wings of birds that promised new beginnings and secrets.

My first stories when I began to write when I was a girl, a child were stories of love; the romantic love that my parents did not give up in our presence as children so I imagined it into reality like Barbara Cartland did in her pink mansion; I imagined it into truth and tricked myself into believing that love was something real; that you could reach out and touch like a gift. I have never believed in Valentine's. Perhaps this was my parents' fault.

What does love mean to me then? An embrace, a kiss, winter rain here again, haiku, leaves softly whispering on the ground, words, words and more words, the terminal at the airport. It is all suspended in mid-air for me like machinery. How much does it take to love? I have realised it is the very essence of your soul, of your being, much of what it takes to write; this is the image that I have of love in my imagination.

At Bible school, I found myself, wisdom, purity, humanity, maturity, alchemy in daily prayer and meditation. In witnessing people, adults, praying in tongues when I could not in the struggle of my life as an adolescent, a skinny teen languishing in sadness and depression; of not being built to fit in with the rest of them; the popular crowd, the girls with boobs. Prayer taught me truth and the truth was that the art for me was not to fail. Failure meant nothing. Prayer grew me up. The desire that I had to be near God meant that emotional maturity beckoned and was not far off. Words buzzed like fizz, and pop in my head.

Unlikely stories, Bible school were my real tools of substance. My instruments, sermons, hymns, my childhood, the divine mysteries of the scriptures. I realised that I could somehow transform essays into miracles on paper. All of the cogs and the wheels that I had at my disposal became my machinery. Madness, chaos, disorder ruled on my desk, in my brain, in my environment. They humbled me; held me captive. I believe that every time I sit down to write it is God's perfect angelic timing but nowadays people do not want to read about God and miracles.

I left Bible school before I finished the apprentice year. I felt I had learned all I could. Before I went I wanted to know why it felt these words just existed for me, passing through, healing my emotions, my hurts, tending to my goals, why they seemed to exist not only for me but for strangers, why I possessed them, how they fell into place windswept, caught beautifully, swept away the lull of the day, gathered harmoniously for a captive audience, built for humanity, they were metallic when I hit them, the sound bouncing around in the elegant, silent rooms of my psyche. These words were a hit. They sparked a revival and a crusade as television evangelists did.

21

The middle-class soul in behavioural therapy

I started to stare in wonder at the world, this unique universe around me. The minister at the side of the road trying to get a lift to only God knows where. Perhaps he was only pretending because he wanted to hitch a ride. Life was easy for me. It was not so easy for other people.

God, adolescent girls, bullies and the Holy Ghost fed the beasts of my imagination.

God did not captivate me in Sunday school. He captivated me in the world, the people, the slamming observations around me, in pale faces and dark ones, in normality and abnormality, children who had Down syndrome, were crippled, or handicapped in some way, the mentally ill, in poetry, as I sat on my father's lap and he stroked my hair.

I adopted the realities of the poet's words I read in my mind. Smelled scents in the night air, the night sky, the emblazoned stars, scent in hair. Without pain, I was blinded. I could not write. I could not see a way through to communicate even simple things. Things of the past that kept me back. A white girl with a halo of blonde hair, with glossy-pink, rubber-pillows for lips who played hockey with thick ankles and sturdy well-built legs and who wore black nail polish on her toes who picked on me daily in the posh high school I went to. I only hoped to break through racial barriers and I think I achieved that. They even gave me an academic award at the end of the year.

It was hellish but I survived. The footprints I carved out there on the steps of those imposing brick buildings prepared me for the future and it taught me that everything I reached out for was within limits and that the past did not determine your future. All I saw around me were rich white girls. They even looked angelic in their school uniforms. The Indian girls were snobs, introverts and cleverer than just about anyone. Their parents were doctors and pharmacists. They came from money.

They never swam when it was physical education. They all had letters from their parents. Adolescence, no matter how painful it was, instructed my writing. The coloured girls lived half-lives. At school they were model scholars, writing down their homework in huge diaries, dutifully studying, acting out whatever the white girls did, speaking like them with posh accents, wore their hair like they did in plaits and bobs and when they went home to their lesser than suburbs, lesser than households they turned wild, went to the shop for bread and milk, wore their hair loose, kissed boys behind the bus stop, held hands, thought reading was boring.

I taught myself to stay calm under pressure; ever watchful under the energy and flow resonating within the crouched limbs of a child navigating the internal; an alien rush for eternity; the essence of a street child's hunger and loneliness. I turned it into a poem.

I feel when I am writing as if I am awake in someone else's dream. Religion was magical but writing made me feel omnipotent. It is demanding. It's gut wrenching. It is a brutal exercise. You're the permanent subordinate while whatever holy ceremony is taking place, stringing the words together into sentences like a rope of pearls switches gears, dropping bombs inside your mind; a mine field.

Intimate ceremonies.

Does it start from the womb? This clamour for attention, this need, this want, this desire to be heard, to be read and to be desired in return? For your words to remain behind as scar tissue, simply read like a ripe fruit on the ground estranged from its brothers and sisters in the orchard hanging from the boughs of trees, like a bleeding slab of red meat, words read out loud on the mat where all the egghead children sit on and read from their readers, enthralling, suffocating, dominating, a country on an atlas or mapped out crazily in crayon in a colouring book, or a geographical location in a school project. Words must nurture like school, like mother, like father, like families at the beach or on holiday, like the books and words of other writers, poets, intellectuals and teachers.

It is not my fingertips that are in authority when it comes to tap-tap-tapping on the keyboard. It is something far more esoteric; something far more intimate and cerebral. It is something that is both lost and found. It is futile for me to say that it comes from within me and me alone, that it comes from the spirit of fear, that this deluge of elegant, elegant language that sums up the ordinary people whose lives are so extraordinary when I put pen to paper, that if I keep a healthy frame of mind; rising like the full moon; like a vision it will come.

I am empowered by the process and all that comes with it; patch its barriers, get sold by boundaries, by borders, by shades of smoke that nestle gravely in the air from old-fashioned pipes and cigarettes. I am only human; a woman. Having a father who suffers from depression, a mental illness, an aunt who suffers from alcoholism and writing frankly about these challenges and their daily challenges has reawakened my calling to service and to writing. I have been called to write, not to minister and not to become a missionary in a far off country like Russia or where it snows and you have to learn to speak a foreign language. A web was lying beneath all of that. I had not learned to shake it off yet. It comes with words; typed, scrawled, handwritten, jotted down hastily before it erases itself like time or a silhouette in sunlight from my memory.

Woman. Writing resurrects me. So what if it comes with wishful thinking, with regret, with verbal ammunition, persecution that consumes you when someone makes a negative comment about something that you have written, that something you can never let go of or surrender; this is it. It is the secret life of dreamers that is kept wanting. I have no doubt in my heart now that this is my career. I have finally come to this understanding. When we pray, we trust God.

When we fall asleep, we know tomorrow when we wake up it will be the next day. Therefore, we will follow the seven days of the week for a year. Just sometimes, I pretend I am a prizewinning journalist or a child at play with war. In my headspace, I am caught by the flow of a river, staring without fear as the current takes me; swallows me up whole in a whirlpool.

God calls to me out of the darkness into the light. I am only released in the precious words in fluid liquid reserved only for the barren landscape, the white ghost of the wilderness of the page. When I first began on this open road, I wrote what my heart was longing for, for a magical home, for magical innocence about the things I once had in my possession, for self-indulgent thinking, for a mother's magical love written magically on my body. I never realised even for an instant that the magic was already inside of me, hidden within the depths of my ego, just waiting to be awakened, pushed opened like a window, a door left ajar, a fence or a gate.

I sit here as the aftertime explodes into life continued. An Iris planting irises. Dirty hands from constant gardening, the bloody-everything of war on the television, in the air, in the newspaper, feet on the stairs, and a stampede in the house of childhood. And I remember the visions I had of men and women, older men and their wisdom and how now their aching vulnerabilities have become much more apparent to me. To insecure, eternally morally bankrupt, withdrawn me. Now my lonely oftentimes humiliating experiences feels like electricity to me. It feels like a rich, beautiful tapestry. The folds are magical. The details angelic like my mother's hair, my lovely sister's hands. She has come home. They have finally both come home to me.

My sister, she is leaving for Bloemfontein after Christmas. I love her so much that it hurts. I don't play the role of an older sister. She's the one with the skills and the role to play even though she's the younger sister (yes, much more skilled sister). She is returning to her cool, calm and collected self. She is returning to the villagers of Johannesburg and all her self-fulfilling prophecies. In the meantime, what happens to the rest of us? There will no longer be any waves of dissension, and you will not be able to cut through the air with a knife. Conversation will not wound. Words will not be sharp and ring in the air. There will be no talk period especially of suicidal illness and the book on the Rivonia Treason trial that my mother stole from the library, hid amongst her other textbooks because she wanted to know Nelson, Kathrada, peace in our time, Winnie, Drum magazine. I could go on but I think I will stop there.

Love changes everything with its dramatic highs and lows. Now I am in my father's wardrobe. I am remembering the feeling-peeling, segment of orange, and tasting the tart juice, all the layers of love I have for him, for his obstinate, sometimes arrogant turn of his head. His suits brush against my arms. Once upon a time, he was some girl's illusion before becoming a spouse, a husband, settling down and raising a family. Young love is a playful kind of love. All I see is a diary of pain, anxiety and madness when it comes to infinite love, the love that you find in a sonnet, resonating in the bond between mother and child, Mary and baby Jesus. All the reckonings of suicidal illness. Not all poetry is poetry without God, substance. Poetry is not poetry without poverty, and spirituality. Without the good things that are born from painful experience.

So the well of loneliness continues in this space, the most personal of spaces and the well has her song. It is a melody whose intuition flows as deeply as any river. We, the reader and the writer have come here and you might be asking yourself now that you have reached this turning point what has been the purpose of leading you up the nowhere with another Christmas story. My sister. She is perfect. She does not need to wash away her sins with organic descriptions, or prescriptions.

She does not wish to visit shamans or old wise men or look upon totem poles only to travel to Peru. Everything about her is extraordinarily pure, a golden state, a garden state and private. It tells me, shows me every day that there can only be one winning woman at the end of the day. There are times when she smiles and something is lit up inside of me like a volcano but I do not lift that veil. I dare not. It is the only time when I remember the time when we were both curious creatures of a childhood where we played at being spiritual overachievers in Sunday school. When we were left to guess the first five books of the Old and the New Testament, taught to leave our ancestors lurking in every silver lining and the dust. Home was the place that other children called safe haven but what kept us

27

anchored in our own was our dystopia, eyeing the vulnerable in others and keeping a look out for that, after finding it holding onto it for dear life (that was me). In addition, I have never stopped doing it.

It is another holiday. It is another lavish affair and an unhurried feast-meal. Nothing unchanged about that only it is another year ending of an interrupted life in an interrupted world (my interrupted life, my interrupted world). She is treated like a slave, a worker-bee, a drone, and I am a zombie untouched by the work ethic that must pull all of this tiger-of-a-holiday together. My beautiful sister is a bright, all-powerful and illuminating glare of nature.

The cat drinks out of a glass of water that has been standing there from the previous evening that I left out next to an apple's core. I made short work of a midnight feast of a glass of water and an apple. Before we sit down to lunch there are telephone calls to get out of the way to family in Johannesburg. The Johannesburg people. Cousins, cousins' children I will never know. I will never watch them grow up, hear them call my name; they will not learn to admire and respect me. Most of all they will not watch me grow old defiantly. In the middle of the lines caught up between the grey areas of madness and despair there is still beauty there but I will never, never have the opportunity of teaching them this. My mother's-love bleeds into my eyes. When I was a child, it was warm, sticky and sweet like Billy Joel's voice on the radio when he sings. Now it is pins and needles, diamonds of stars in the sky and now all I hear is her voice telling me that there is room for my gift in the world too. It is as if we are seeing the river, the novel wave, the wave, its burden for the first time, afresh, purified like a Catholic ritual.

Vodka for the pain. It is fragile up there. There is a faraway storm, an emotionally damaged gene pool in every battle study, an angel tongue, for every weaving of a scream there is a lucid one. There is a stem, a Jacob's ladder, a lover, a mother, an orphan, a wife, a constant gardener who has what it takes to build muscle in a mysterious, intriguing world.

You weave the awful, the terrible things that happened to you as a child into a story. You remember the bonds of family, the pathways to the familiar, the horrors of the sexual assault against her as a child, fighting the grave monsters within, and human suffering, injustice, waves of finding intimacy in the moveable feast of the sexual transaction. There is horror in intimacy too. When we find it, we usually look away. The brutality of man against man, that raw, animalistic anger, that walk and the fact that we must remind ourselves of who we are every day and just how much memory work that takes to roost, to brood, to reject, to pour ourselves into every ritual, wash away every sin. It seems as if all her life she has been in the pursuit of histories, love and prayer.

The light illuminates everything around her, the ghosts from her present to her past and the future ones, there is a sadness to the day as if all the world's burdens are upon it, another holocaust, another genocide, another otherworldliness. She is guarded and withdrawn. Her last love affair ended badly and now she must make up for it. She takes long walks either alone or with her father. She has come home. The wind is up and so is her mood but she knows it won't be for long until history catches up with her, the frustration of suicidal illness, mental illness, the stigma of it in the community, amongst her estranged family, feeling lost without the history of courage and prayer in the wilderness. Decay has broken out from the stem of her heart and all around her are volcano people.

She listens to them in a daydream day in and day out. She cannot go back to Johannesburg. She cannot go back to Swaziland. She cannot go back to Cape Town. There is no longer family there, threads that can connect her to her old life and besides she was always on the verge of a nervous breakdown when she was there. It is so cold now but the sun is still there, up-in-the-platter-of-the-sky, shining for what it was worth. Her mood veered from pensive to anxious (a separation anxiety). The rain has come and there is no longer dry soil in which nothing can grow or flower, the burning sand at the beachfront is gone, children do not play outside with their bicycles, quad bikes and balls, they have all gone inside. She does not hear their voices, their screams, laughter. Her brother is outside smoking. The more that he reveals himself she discovers that he is not so tough-rough-around-the-edges and she feels sorry for him, sorry for his girlfriend, sorry for her family and most of all sorry for his angelic son.

And she thinks to herself if she ever does it, kills herself will she leave the car running, slit her wrists, jump off a bridge, hang herself or take an overdose of sleeping pills. She does not take it seriously though. She knows she would never do it. It is not because she is not brave enough; she just does not have it within her. She talks a big talk like the comfort she gets from strangers, their velocity. Once in a house on fire always in a house on fire. She always wanted to be surrounded by men. Their feverishly brilliant power, their scrapbooking intelligence and she was under the idea that somehow it would patch up her childhood and lonely adolescence. They were the ones who taught her poetry (how fresh and novel it could be), the bewildering movement of the memoir, the dynamic art of film and how it could give her a lifeline, anchor her buoyantly. However, it took her a long time to realise she was never the exclusive one. In addition, when she did it shattered something like glass within her.

30

When you are broken when, how and where do you go from there? When you realise there are children in the picture and perhaps other lovers too. All her life she had been unafraid even of the sexual impulse in man and other women but then accidents began to happen all the time. A lot began to happen around her. Arguments, derisive comments in the workplace, the sexual harassment (boys being boys thinking that women were just toys, playthings, that young, tall, wallflower, inexperienced temporary worker). In Johannesburg she did not eat, she could not sleep at night; she tossed and turned turning over visions of the day in her head.

The sexual disorder, how she told herself repeatedly that there were no things such as ghosts but she still put the sheet over the mirror that looked like a river at night. A river that could reveal faces scissoring through the dark blue air and tell stories. Everything was bittersweet about Johannesburg, darkly blank, ghosts swimming, ghosts surfing resurfacing and she was the poised quiet woman, the sinner that moved from room to room until to the end of the world. Cape Town was a very, very lonely place but in Swaziland she met up with good citizens, young people, old people, children, black faces, white faces, brown faces.

Hair with different texture, straight, ironed, curly, relaxed with chemical treatments, blonde. They all had enchanting faces the girls and boys, enchanting accents, came from all over Africa. An Africa she had never seen or heard of before. They all seemed to live idyllic lives in this green feast of rolling hill after rolling hill and twisting valleys. This was the empire of exotic coloured high school swans. The older sky until winter infiltrated it. For the first time she saw snow. She loved the night in Swaziland. It left her breathless, on the warpath with scars, poems about her mother and the wild sea of Port Elizabeth.

Wilderness was a wilderness. Her family and she went to a church there, stayed at a hotel, never went near the beach, and spent most of their time in the swimming pool or on the tennis court. The chlorine burned her eyes. Her brother and she would go swimming at night seeing how long most of the time who could hold their breath the longest under water. George was a widow's song. It was a sad town. She did not like the energy there. Then there was her other life. The opposite of sex. Elizabeth Donkin, Hunterscraig, Tara, Valkenburg and Garden City Clinic. The source of everything. Madness, despair, darkness, nightmares, scar tissue, her adventures in the silent night, in the light of day, yonder and the devil. All the girls she has ever met in her life are bone girls who have probably become bone women.

Writing through disability, illness and chronic fatigue

No ghost of terminal illness or chronic disease have they. Their blood is clean like the head of an exile child. They are not wounded in any way. They do not speak with their hands, with that slight tremor that comes with the taking of Epilizine. There were men in her family who drank and women in her family who drink and how they all bordered on the wilderness history, us women with our cold hands, our cold feet and their madness. It is our men, our people, women who have taught us to discard our values like the emperor's new clothes and to drink (to drink as they do, to drink them under the table). She thought to herself.

Iris's Journal entry

Was I not the best little girl in the world? Spoilt yes but why do we have to grow up so fast? I really have let myself go in a dream sequence. I eat thirds of everything. Beautiful girls were his great enduring love. My great enduring love's love. Once you, you bright eyes were my muse, texture like sun and what a precious cargo you were. Only you fell among the stars never to return. My frankincense and myrrh. Therefore, I am left in mourning while you pass me by, a fragile beauty. I am left with my dope-smoking addict of a brother, with his cigarettes, stale smoke and moustache for male company. Ashtray filled with cigarette ends. The years have changed us into people we do not find familiar in any way. Brothers and sisters. Our lives are defined by whom we are, memories, marked by trials, mine promiscuity.

The pulse is a parachute opening and closing, shutting its mouth. The practical magic of it all. I will always remember the memory of love. It will never shut me out. I love my brother like I love my great enduring love, the pursuit of him was always bordering on wilderness and madness. There is darkness even in an echo. A movement of the creator in solitude that lingers and in that moment I am holding onto nothing. There is blues in a cold street. If I trace its breaking point, I come across the eternity of the primitive impulse. The sea river is a cold impasse. Will I find secrets there? In my dream, I am standing on a frozen lake, the second sex and I can hear female voices all around me. Some are comforting just like a prayer as if to give me the courage of my convictions.

In addition, I get the feeling that they are teaching me the elementary wisdom of survival skills. Nevertheless, the voice of my one true love is no longer heard. No longer golden. No longer the voice of a male writer. As foe or beautiful it is not just enough to exist anymore. I have to find a way out of this celestial madness. However, trust me it can be good for the bones like Paris. I wish I had a dress that I could go anywhere with but I am not one of those girls who purge their unhappiness like that. All I want is a childhood continued swarming, magnetic, like spiritual children attracting like. What has become of me, what will become of me in this ghost nation? The child comes to me. His mother gives him to me. I do not know why they trust me with him. I feel I can hurt him the way I was hurt as a child. Edward.

He is precious, innocent. I gave him that name. He sits on my lap. My brother's son. He is sucking his fingers. He has long lashes and dark brown eyes like his father. He is pretty. He is as pretty as a girl is. He has eczema on his neck. Every night and morning after his bath, his mother rubs aqueous cream into the inflamed parts of his peeling skin. His face is white-pale like snow, a moon, a cloud with a silver lining. You can see he has Germanic ancestry. He is two months old. Edward smiles at me. There is a supernatural energy from his unyielding gaze. Love changes everything for the sinner, the return comes with it, the immortal, and so does bright fame. Fish. Fish and chips. The survival kit for life is eating, in food, food for thought, food that nurtures the body. I breathe in the lemon wedge, white fish and the vinegar.

I want to be normal like Alice in her electronica trippy wonderland. I grace. Daddy bows his head. The bones of this year has left us with much breathing lessons. I want to swim away from the tigers. In the morning daddy exercises while I drink my lukewarm coffee. Sometimes tea. Sometimes coffee. I have to watch him now. I have to watch over him now. He could double over. He could fall. He could wet himself. Yesterday we laughed-and-laughed-and-laughed at Marc Lottering this famous South African comedian and that is what we do as a family these days. We laugh, we smile, we hug Edward, and we breathe in. We watch sex, lies and videotape. What are we trying to forget, trying to forgive, where do we go from here? We eat sleeping pills, medication that can be bought over the counter.

Melatonin, Pax and Ativan, multivitamins like layers of wedding cake and I hope that God forgives us. God has given us Edward, a blessing-in-disguise, isn't a child always the first wave of consciousness? I am reminded of Jesus and the Pharisees when I look at him. The blood orange sky that I wrote about once in a poem about me and my brother, Auschwitz, Bergen-Belsen (what the experiment of evil was once in Nazi-Germany (their-guinea-pigs-white-mice-in-a-maze), SS soldiers saluting Hitler, his moustache, German youth and what they're still capable of). Edward reminds me of Roman Polanski of all people, Woody Allen's films (vignettes of my life), his love affair and muse Mia Farrow. There are so many paths that are open to Edward, our little prince. I pray that all the love letters that roll from my heart can help navigate his journey a little bit more as he grows older. In his eyes, I forget time, burnt diaries, midnight, and Rilke's Paris.

I forget that I am growing older. One day I will be an old woman.

She has now taught her son to be a constant gardener. My mother has sacrificed. The world has given me her back. Every Technicolor, flawed, hallucinogenic, schizophrenic muscle in modern society has given her back to me. She is my sun, my heat, my pouring rain, my high, my low. I must not give up because this siren is the one who sustains me, pulls me through.

Even in the heightened realities of nucleic acid, bodily fluids, human stains, case studies, identity theories what it all comes down to is this really. Family is family, and we all belong to the human race, a human family. Now we come to love again and we approach it from a different angle. It can give us so much glory, pleasure; it can take us from the paradise of heaven to the stairways and wards of hell.

I am at the gates, the city streets behind me, the history of violence, silence, loneliness is a shell like suffering, sanity, the bittersweet aftertaste of alcoholism, my brother 'locked' behind the gates in rehab, the passing death of someone close in the family. Magda, Magda, Magda shining star that I am still addicted to like gravity, halo above the lost tug of an ocean sea of emotions wherever you are now. I will never let go completely of you.

36

I am home. I am flying. I am dreaming. I am a vessel and even though in some of my dreams there is an accumulation of emptiness housed there. So this year Christmas was not completely ruined. I was not torn. There were not raised voices behind closed bedroom doors.

Now we come to exploring the form of the memoir. However, perhaps this is not the flowery exit you have come to expect because when love is up for discussion then so is the plan of departure, chemistry. A book a year is not enough for me anymore. The bite of a story with a human face a week is what I live on.

I have lived even though you do not believe it. I have loved even though you do not believe it. Think of my love life, my life so far as tragedy speeded up if you will. Do not pause. Do not think. The weight of water was never the enemy in the sea or swimming pool with the chlorine burning my eyes. Every stroke towards the wall (whether it is the wall of the horizon in the distance or the opposite wall of the pool is a small goal achieved). It is a leap of faith. I pour my roots into a feast. The stems of me.

Say you remember. I think of him. My winter's sadness. My heart is suffering. We have not even kissed yet. However, I remember how alive I felt with his arms around my waist. His dark hair wet at the nape of his neck means more to me than sensuous imagery. He is dangerous. He can ruin me, my reputation and he has and so have I. I am an intern. He is something else. With him, I am a goddess, desired and beautiful. Bitterness no longer cuts through me hot and blistering. Without him, I am a god, a little female impersonation of the Buddha. He is a dream. He is a memory. Silence has grown between us all through these years. I would not be here if it were not for you. Writing to reach American you. I do not have a Christmas party dress. I see to my father. His needs and not 'the man-about in the office'. His medication, his pharmacy, his meals, making his coffee, helping him dress in the morning, evening, and I have found a newer, brighter shape of love. I have discovered its elements are more authentic than sometimes the dryness of writing, and the sensuality of the therapy of cooking. To some thirty year old me this means motherhood.

He (the-man-about-the-ice) has never looked more beautiful in the pictures of my mind. I needed him to forget about childhood, adolescence, every past Christmas. He makes my mind and heart race. He makes me think international. I need to win. I need him now. He is my first love and as I grow older and sense I will never meet him in my future-men he is my only love. Now his eyes, his laugh, his smile, the dimensions of his clothes, his wuthering height strikes me thin. This is my life now. The past becomes fresh, the present mean and the future does not seem to build up to a future of the rewards of big dreams.

Here are the elegant questions. Where is the connection? What is love when it occurs in humanity's first catalyst? It is merely a survival instinct shooting straight from the first spirited heartbeat after falling. Even a hard man with his cunning and his brutal ways can win a 'sexual transaction', and a woman with her pretty ways, even a silly woman can win a man if she is feminine. Now we look at the prostitute, the promiscuous, the socialite and what do all of them have in common. Everyone is lonely. Everybody hurts. Everybody is fighting from the con man and con woman is fiercely intelligent because everybody has to live. Are we all truly born equal, is freedom in our land nothing more than a psychological construct, what separates the rich and the poor, the talented in their own right, the introverted leader and the gifted and savant from the ordinary? Those with an equal share of darkness, the criminal in them have to fight for the dark world, those forces to overcome their authentic godliness. Their goodness. The voluptuous light within them.

It is Christmas. Everyone is home. I remember my first love as we sit down to eat. He lives in another world filled with normal, sanity, convenience, discretion, a wife and a child who has a horse. I am no longer afraid, ashamed of walking away instead of towards the brilliant eye of the storm (sleeping with the enemy). I do not orbit the world of powerful men, star people anymore. My mind has changed. It is charged, wired with calculations about what other people are doing, thinking and the harmonic cultures that exist outside of my own. It has been years since I have entertained, left those playing fields. Less than a golden decade has passed, and my feelings for most of them. I am a woman now.

My ministry has changed, opinion, point of view. I sit with my mother, my sister, my brother, his pregnant girlfriend and my father I feel blessed. I have a journey, a Plan B, a mission, love, family. Another year. Look at all of us. Some of us have become more introspective than others. We are all soldiers every one of us. We each have our own psychological makeup that cuts us deep seriously, political ideas, and philosophy about life.

There is something about the monk in all of us.

None of us know how much time we have left

It feels like winter in September and the skies are just supposed to be pieces of blue but instead they're slate grey with the beckoning, darkening rain clouds not yet completely rinsed out of them. My sister and I do not have a perfect relationship.

We are not close and when it comes to the question of God, we are as far apart as Cassiopeia from the planes and landscapes of this planet. I wonder what the devil has got into her and console myself with the fact that all demons are spirit. They are not forces to be reckoned with only negative thoughts. I cannot take that haunting divide that lies between us away. I cannot wish it away. Wish it gone into air; wish its legacy deceased. So I walk away, navigate the swollen crossroads and pathways of letters on the spines of books searching for something all consuming; that will take up my precious time.

I just got off the phone now, talking to her, trying to control my voice as hers went higher and higher. I was calling to tell her about our father and how disoriented he has become. I have even become aware that there are symptoms of Alzheimer's. I do not know what to do. I do not know what I am supposed to feel or do anymore. I am left wondering just how unfair life is now.

All she does is take leaving the details and lines of the shape of my heart hopelessly mismatched and in denial. Just the day before we were laughing as if we were best friends, all she wanted was a boyfriend; she spoke about flirting at her office and the number of men who asked her to go out for coffee. I wish she were more dedicated to family life, instead of shutting herself out and becoming withdrawn when shapes of negativity come up. Perhaps my inconsistent misbehaviour is to blame for this when I was growing up. Therefore, she speaks to me as if she birthed me even though I am older than she is.

My spine turns to jelly, as if someone's cool fingers are playing Bach on it. I am mad with grief; slowly going insane as if the juices of the fat are not the way I want it to; dissolving, melting into curves and circles into the potatoes next to the roast in the oven. In everything I did since I was an infant I took instruction, gathered it from my father. Words like 'erudite', 'perusal'. I picked up 'jargon' and 'verbose' from one of my favourite teachers who also happened to be my principal when he took our English classes when our normal teacher was absent.

My sister and I had never whispered secrets to each other breathlessly under the covers of a camp made in the family room out of pillows, blankets, and seats that we removed from the armchairs. Instead, we watched films and she followed me in my footsteps in studying it further after high school. Instead of being a documentary filmmaker now, she works in a bank.

There is a rumpus in my head. My mother's ovaries are exhausted. My father's voice a peeling ceiling and my grief over his condition goes unnamed. It is a splash of red; a keen, stunned abortion of small nothings.

I watch old black and white movies: Casablanca, Now Voyager and Night of the Iguana; I drink lavender sweet vine with my version of the Mona Lisa on my lips, I am caught up; predatory, psychic - it is not the first time I hear the word 'intense'. I am described as being emotional. I wonder at the self-awareness of it all, its delicate design foisted upon me, I question its authenticity, God ceases at once.

Choose me, I say all angelic, I pull through nausea; the origins lie in novel, candid translations. I hear the croaking of a frog when I go

41

to sleep just outside my open window – in the morning it is gone, shut up into a literary space, belly full of rumpus, neck restrained, a baby's crying voice in the night air from the house next door. All this attention comes slow motion, riles me; alerts me to the battalions of flitting, whitish moths overhead, their seed pulped against the walls of the lit bathroom, a sniffing dog on neighbourhood watch howls to the moon, scratches itself, a flea's temple of delight.

I am not yet in need of self-help, there are more needful things at hand that I have to deal with I give my neuroses, my pangs the cold shoulder; the pupils of my eyes dead to the world. I ask, hinted at war children, schools of fish to come to me.

Standing at the water's edge at the local swimming pool human bodies' poke out of the water, limbs akimbo, loaded, they float on the water in the pool faces fluid, pure, relevant. My father's quiet footsteps in the early hours of the morning come with shifty bliss; order in chaos.

There was writing and education; a knowing factual atlas, he came with a prescription for anti-depressants, hustle and fuss. Three babies brought up together, mirror images of each other packing an alluring shameless stage, a censored shopping list knitted out with pharmaceuticals, kitted out with it; shelved under the tongue of a brother and two sisters. The knives are out, insomnia grazes our brains; tell me what you want to hear, a feast of gossip?

What am I supposed to do now since my mother put a stop to it, she touched the nape of my neck? When I said I have taken as much as I could take I moved into focus, into view, understood the trials of motherhood. Her trials that she went through with me that I could never fathom before; how it killed her to see me wasting my potential in a hospital full of restless crazies. I remember her perfume and how she fingered her wedding band. How she wore her hair down and

42

how it brushed in a fashionable bob against her shoulders. How inside I felt so terrified that she was leaving me behind because she could not 'handle this' anymore. I failed her.

I remember how I could see pieces of blue sky from the bars on my window. Vincent van Gogh painted it, lived it and every part of his physical, emotional and spiritual being was consumed by it. I was not far behind. As the depression lingered so did my guilt. My insomnia rivalled it. Getting sleep was like a present; feeding the beasts inside.

He saw me first.

Fractured, embellished, setting a precedent, drowning in misery, depression, the loveliness of honestly gained happiness; it imprisoned me, healed my old wounds, old things, fashioned the new, shooting into the hemispheres of my brain, blinded me, made me realise that the negative self is not the real self.

Our love was a love that was fleeting, that came in sublimely playful and adventurous and pained instalments; the only difference was that he was white and I was coloured. He was a sad and beautiful creature who could cut me with ease with a word that sliced through the air. I did yet not have the mental toughness I have now so I often ended up in tears, blinking them back as I did with the lump in the cave of my throat. He could silence me with a look. All I wanted was to be loved and for him to daily message that to me

He could be fun but also a sullen beast.

There were days when our relationship felt like it was a long journey. It nourished me, it spoiled me (some days I was adored,

43

others I was abhorred), it made me militant, gave me guidance that spoke to my inner core; so what, if one day we were kindred spirits and the next at war with each other.

He had his own ways and means of getting under my skin. I was just happy that he paid attention and that he listened. He had his own moods. I had mine. Together, when he was up and I was down we drew blood, lines on the ground of whose territory belonged to whom.

We were crossing the subtle barriers of race. Interracial relationships were then fraught with anxious poses in the new South Africa. It is hard to remember what other people thought of us when I look back. It was so many things. It was hard to erase that it felt both alien and like home when I was rooted in his arms.

I could memorise all the times we had fallouts. We never really dated, we just hung out. We never held hands or went to the movies. What we did was talk a lot about everything. His head told me I spoke a language he could not understand. I wrote to him. I wrote him long, passionate letters that spoke of a girl's love. I could never be as forthcoming face to face. I would bare my soul in these letters to the very last drop and then bestow it in his lap as a gift. He never wrote back. This should have told me something in the early days but I was wrapped up, transformed by someone who could so easily make me smile and laugh at myself.

He was ruthless at doing that.

Sometimes they were about the grief I felt, the negativity and insecurities I felt so deeply, that moved within my gut that never seemed to dissolve or grow weaker no matter how much he touched me and reminded me of the dysfunctional, loving, father with the soft

44

heart, neurotic mother; home of my childhood that I left behind; a home that I could have sweet memories of.

Once I surrendered to the unknown, his beautiful bones I was caught in his tender poise. He was not willing to give me more but I was more than willing to put my enchanted, productive heart into it; to give it place and function. I was mesmerised by the dewy stars, sparks in his eyes that made me shiver.

Now I recall it was just a phase that we were both passing through, maturing in healthy patterns, we were moving in layered circles, growing older, learning from each other and naturally on towards other burgeoning destinations; other relationships with women and men when it was over.

Of course, in the mean time before the relationship between us cooled, he grew colder, meaner, humiliated me; this is what happens in all relationships between a girlfriend and a boyfriend when one is dominated by the other. It hurt. Our world soon became a cell. I could see a patch of blue sky through the bars but there was no escape.

Growing up I was taught to generate a feeling of hate towards whites. They had, we did not.

I only could dream about eliminating the tension between us; thought his only mission was to break me down.

He was my first everything. I shadowed all the kinks in his armour. I drew strength from him.

I learnt a lot about life, about the source of love that it takes a lot of discipline and practice and that the world has no power before the power of God. I believed we were two outcasts in an unforgiving and hostile world.

Years to figure that final analysis out

He reminded me of red heat, and dust under a pale sun. He loved to tan. He loved surfing. He was and came from a part of the world that was foreign to me. In return he gave me solace; moments to be by myself; with my precious words that I was just discovering.

He read my letters and then gave them back to me when I asked for them; when we were through.

He is only a ghost now; written on the body, my spine, the river of my back, the scent of his head on a pillow, between sheets, a bedspread, his warm mouth on my skin lost in high speed, not following or thinking or allowing for a plan. There is only a peace of mind that affords me some rest now on the past.

Writing poetry has become my cognitive therapy. Although, it is a lonely activity it keeps me sane away from the hungry memories of my sister and the ghost of my first love. Technically, now my first love is words, language stretched out like the elastic bands of calamari that I spoon from the plate to my mouth with my oily fingers.

I live in the present moment; safe from the harm of his memory; battle scarring, emotional wounding. We were so far from being a suitable fit anyway. He is no longer familiar neither are his fingers; me clinging to him for fear that I would lose sight of him, of my sister, lose my hold, my grasp on him, shut upped by her ringing voice and so I shuttle in the in-between. My arbitrary common sense tells me so.

For as long as I can remember I have talked to the dead, spirits that have passed on to the hereafter and in that after time I housed collections of every kind, blank pages as clean and pure as milk, the estate of moths, my useful tools frigid like the weather, stunned, shrouded fakes during all seasons. The light, wood in the forest swallows me completely. Everything has been harder even the planetary lentils. Their name is beautiful and black-pitted, veiled in the pot; their continent and in their honeymoon there are open roads. There are no boundaries, no ghost-pillars; the feast of ocean and the wild sky. As they split open on my tongue, these cathedrals that was once as hard as stone become cauldrons, unflinching masters. I need nerves of steel here over the steam escaping from cooking pots; a wonderland of Basmati rice and chicken curry. We grew up fast. There was church, school, and afternoon activities and then there was our house; our home, our parents, our family, where the roots of a supreme cover-up began.

The silent sea under the pier at Shark Rock in Port Elizabeth I imagine must feel like ice and I can feel myself slipping, between the waves welcoming folds, drowning in this watery landscape of a small town setting becoming a flailing half-drowned thing, the ocean's skin on my skin. If only I had not grown up wild, heard all these words inside my mind like pine or willow trees, heard their music gel like the song of wind sweeping through the branches in a desolate forest, multiplied with the unbearable lightness of the features of my serotonin and dopamine and wondered what seed would embed itself comfortably in that heady space of wild blue sky; the seed that was words? I have turned myself perfectly into this wintering where I am an uninvited guest. With this self-knowledge comes joy and the emptiness of loneliness and childhood hurts, opening myself up to possibilities.

In melancholy, I am locked in a quaint, inventive state of mind like animals captured and paraded in zoos or portraits of every generation.

I refuse to die here. Instead, I lay on my bed, covered with the bedspread. I pretend I cannot get up today, I cannot move, stir from this place. On every branch, every leaf sighs dew, intact bubbles of purified water. If I squeeze it with a finger, it oozes like a spasm, like blood falling, before the bubble melts. The conflict that is inside every man is the same conflict inside of me. How to make contact with a vital, young woman who is as visible as stone and the conflict within me is how to be that woman, unquestioning, imaginative, aware of how to create, to create children but it is a pointless exercise at my age. Perhaps if my mouth was still shut up like a door or a brick wall like it was in my youth I would have more hope, then there would be more hope for me.

How sweet lukewarm hot chocolate milk tastes when the wind is up, sometimes hollering, sometimes just banging incessantly against the windows, caught in my hair as I give the dog food and fresh water in the twilight watching the new moon. How sweet my parents would have been in the beginnings of wedded bliss playing house. I buy and arrange furniture flying solo. No science, proof of life, Dadaist instruction given to me to grow reed-thin, to grow as tall as a ladder, to beam me into another dimension, a reality where I wasn't baffled or having to voice the thin red line running through it, the river of fat teeth, the river of tides, the river of mercy, of fat Buddha statues that was my life. I am left guarded, holding my breath under water; the water of the ocean-sea, wearing a green mask that tastes of salt, a ghost with a long memory of perfume, watermelon on a sandy beach, sunshine beating down on my shiny head and smiling in another country. In photographs, pictures as a family we made a cold diagram, our faces launched forever into oblivion in the frames of the negatives with our crooked smiles, gaping teeth. The only thing that I found comforting was our wide-eyed innocence for all the world to see and the fact that we could not blink, see the routes we would end up following. Anxious even as children when we were pulled apart at the threads, sobriety set us in a rhythm that never failed. We painted smiles as soft as velvet as children on our faces, squinted in the white sunlight. Poor us, poor tarnished jewels on this growing conscience of a planet, of a continent. How fragile we were in our small town setting.

What they could not see was the glow of the beguiling machinery that built us. All its internal cogs, whistling relics, traps, wheels, hearts made of stone built to last bloodlines and bombs; the external hush that followed us into adulthood ambushes us at every turn.

Why can't wintering between glaciers be sweet instead of a Mecca in an age of iron? Why does it have to be a lesson, lines in a blood knot, a blot on the landscape that leaves me thrilled and bedazzled wanting more? Then shutting out death until it is no longer present or hostile, putting out its feelers for barbarism for life.

You, my brother, older, grown up, turned in an ocean of beads. Your eyes were ice. I am cold in sleep just a body quietly curled up with a belly filled with tuna fish sandwiches and hot, authentic vanilla chai made from tea bought in India where my sister spent Christmas and New Year 2009. I am feeling like waves in dark waters picking at their own feast. A woman like me stays in place shut up like a mountain. I give this to you. This language inside your flat where you fit but I do not, I fit badly wherever my sister fits perfectly, but you refuse it, to have that would mean the death of you and bad luck. Now you are testing me with a knife. How it glints with its own just reward in my mind's eye. Just prick me with the needle; I want to say, wishing it so and be done with it. Apparently, no nurse has to burn as I do. I watch how she moves, pivots, turn, points it and the pattern imprinted on skin. She could beat me with a stick and I, the outsider of the family, the writer and the poet would not feel anything. Certainly not the weak pulse in every unforeseen gesture of my blood. I need my rest. They say I have climbed enough brick walls, licked enough ceilings and then suddenly I am falling into air without a sound out of nowhere fast. Reality is all speeded up; its rock face's habitat, its seduction theory. I have done well to keep this to myself before this motion goes haywire or concealed. There stands a foot not yet six feet under, not yet rot. There is something noble about it. It has that kind of air about it. Does it belong to a director, a visionary or a saint? It would be madness on my part to say I recognise its paleness and the bare heels. This is my punishment; to be called lazy, mad, to be called a lunatic and to be rushed around. Is she hearing voices, the system, the establishment, my own mother will ask? Take her to the clinic or the private hospital, they say, so I have heard. However, it has been said and not been said in my presence. They will see to her. They will see to all her needs. A nurse will see to it that she eats. She will peck at it; my pure doppelganger, whatever is plated in that country to death.

Of angels and aliens, interlopers and misanthropes

Melancholy is the blood of my blood, rushing through my veins, splintering off, veering hastily in different directions with its fat teeth. It is bound in the cities of dark waters. It runs with the aid of the moon, birds in flight, carrion, smitten-fog, lizards and there's so much plain life apparently embedded in them; in handfuls beneath skies that refuse to die. In this country, you can taste dust on air, words of a secret poet and writer. Where were the episodes of tension, the ripples? They were there when I was opening a tin of pilchards, when my sister was making us supper again, cutting up pieces of meat, dicing potatoes, opening up a packet of soup to make a gravy to go with the stew for a broken-hearted father, an emotional mother, a withdrawn older sister who fell asleep every night with the light on; a middle child; a sister, always caught in the middle who smelled like yoghurt and honey and a brother who as he grew older became alluring to all types of women. He is darker than the rest of us with his cropped hair and his eyes. There is just too much wintering going on in his eyes these days and it pierces my heart to bits and pieces; like when my broken-hearted father was sick in the hospital and we, the four of us, didn't know if he was literally going to make it or not. My mother did not cry. She did not make pots of tea, tear her hair out instead, she meditated, went to prayer meetings, went to church and ignored the fact that my father was sick and that the rest of us were sick with worry.

My father was so ill in fact that the doctors had intimated that he was on his deathbed and that perhaps as a family we would have to prepare for this. Nobody that we knew of came to the house, came to the hospital to see him because this was in Port Elizabeth and as far as my father's family was concerned my mother was persona non grata and if she was persona non grata then so was my father and my brother, my sister and me. While my mother ignored it into oblivion and there 'it' stayed, he recovered and everyone said it was a miracle. Instead of talking, we ate. We bought toasted cheese and tomato on whole-wheat bread sandwiches at a café just outside the hospital after visiting hours in the evening and ate it the car on the way home. I cooked, while I did that for the two of us, my mother planted fruit trees, blushing rosebushes and put antheriums into pots, pansies, lavender and herbs in her garden. By now, my brother and sister were living in another city, working hard, going out with their friends at the weekend. Eating for me felt good. It made me want to live. We ordered takeaways, pizza over the telephone that could be delivered to our home, ate fish and chips with lashings of brown vinegar and coleslaw. My mother and I walked barefoot on the beach. I did not get to know her better. I did not get a chance to get to know her, as she was when she was a girl or a youth. During this time, I did not ask her anything, question her about her history, instead I wrote poetry with a passion and saturated the blue lines on paper with words buzzing with an intensity of light and energy. It made up for the passion I did not feel coming from the union of my parents, my sister's coldness towards me; it helped me with some recovery from the universe around me, it helped me imagine, kept me from the wolves, kept them more and more at bay. Eating was like the creation of poetry; preparing and laying the table, fork on the left hand side, knife on the right and glass in the corner of the plate, a jug of water on the table filled with blocks of ice tinkling against the side of the jug and filled with slices of lemon or cucumber. We even imagined we were eating a feast even if it was only rice and lentils, what the proper Indians of Durban, of anywhere in Africa called, 'dhal'. As I grew older, wiser, more emotionally grounded, settled, mature, set in my own, determined ways; as my brother began to settle himself in his work and the world around him, as our loyalty to each other became stronger, I began to see myself in other writers and poets work. I was slowly fashioning myself after them, educating myself, learning, processing English, the language and I knew, I knew I could never bring children into this world and subject them to the warm, ceremonial womb of blue seed that the local swimming pool was to me, a sanctuary, where I couldn't hear the raised voices of mother and father arguing back and forth, fighting it out behind their closed bedroom door. I just did not have that kind of tough fight within me.

A writer inspired by Rilke, Hemingway, Fitzgerald and Orwell

There are men in this world, then there are women (it does not really matter what kind they are), and then there is me, the girl who has never completely grown up. There is something of an 'Alice in Wonderland' or the better half of Peter Pan about me. I am entirely lovely at first it seems. Vulnerable, I have depth, there is a poignant sadness in my eyes yet I remain inherently pure. Arrogance and pride can never quite venture near the insecurity of a youth, the gamine. There is nothing about the word sex object that can be traced back to me. If I am stained by anything, it is lipstick and coconut oil on my hands (for my hair). In the hair salon women stand around me braiding my hair exclaiming the prowess of their men, eating hake from the chippy at the corner shop, doing my nails. I already feel a fraud as if nature is ganging up on me. This is not me. This is not who I am or want to be. However, do I want to be 'Alice' forever? One day I will be too old to remember any of these things. Nevertheless, I have already learnt that love releases you from wounds, turns salt into gold.

I was after his flesh and his spirit. You see God in love could keep his soul. Love poured out of me like a sonnet even while I heard his voice in my head like a mixed tape masterpiece that I could hit replay on all the time. 'You're a child that needs to be supervised, told what to do, placated, a docile, docile child. So how can you mother my children if you are a child? How can you be a wife if you didn't have a mother, some mother-figure, a feminine role-model?' He was the one who found me destitute in squalor, in poverty of the spirit, identity and the mind living on the street. He wrecked my psyche, my ego and it was years before I could finally let go of him. The relationship was bittersweet. It taught me that everything in life worth longing for and holding onto is fragile. It served as a reminder that now I am tired of the cold. Cold men with their cold hands tying the threads of my heart together shutting light, all sensibility out, gathering those threads, gathering them like hunters in the wild.

That is the trouble with growing up, getting older. The world gets meaner, men and women and even sometimes children get meaner if you do not play by the rules of the game. I mean the world at large can be a miserable nation with shark teeth ready to rip and pull at any moment. In addition, when that rug of love is pulled out from under you whether you are a child playing in the dirt or a child playing in love your spirit can become dispossessed, lost, displaced. Men, their hands could feel like moss, wind, or winter, water in a spring. Women were a different kettle of fish. I tried to catch them but they danced in a rush, sprinted out of my grasp. They had their own needs, which meant they had their own children, pressures, depression, sadness; they had to place their own disorders and homes in order. They did not want me to call them 'mother'. I have taken the 'inner me' beyond and back. When I make contact with its imaginary blueprint it is a pretty picture reminiscent of a constellation.

I see stars diamond-bright. I see illusion in everything around me, people's facial expressions, their hand movements, the physical, emotional and then the imagination, the pictures it comes from, perhaps a childhood frozen in time. I see illusion even in the beauty of men. In their physicality and the momentum, which drives them to succeed, to climb ladders of distinction with audacity, which leaves the precocious child, starved for their dominion. I was once (and some parts of me, the innocence longs dearly for that dominion to fill up my lovely bones) that precocious child. I still have that spirit and that spirit seeks out its mirror image. The male image that is of a protector, caretaker and in some ways a nurturer. But also a destroyer to sabotage the purity in the head of that precocious child and so when I was twelve years old I did my best not to make any sort of long-term plans and I think for that I have paid a terrible price. I have felt anxious all my life.

My mother the sun, my father the moon both not smiling. Anxiety could do that to you when you came from nothing but a sleepy city that had fish and chippy shops all around at the bay and boats from all over the world that docked in the harbor. It, anxiety could rub off on you when you were having your best moment in the spotlight, academic achievement. I am tired of winter. There are things such as ghosts and if I am going to survive then I have to study the survival of other artists, women, the female mystic and poet, the feminine. I am not a woman; I am not a warrior, a mother, a wife, and not even a girlfriend. I am a child again and an innocence and purity sticks. Therefore, I curl up on the sofa with my legs beneath me leaning my back against the back of it, brushing hair out of my face, wishing the blues away. I am twelve years old again. High school is so fresh it is in my pores. It makes me feel dizzy.

So dizzy that it is sometimes hard to breathe, hard to eat, hard to react to the world around me. Hard to see how much work it takes to make popular reality and to define just what that means. It means I do not have to make any plans yet. I am bored and the only thing that interests me is war, television, the history that Martin Luther, and Martin Luther King comes with, Bunsen burners and the periodic table. Life is bittersweet at twelve years old. My mother is sweet, talking her way into some deal with my father. In the photograph, I am holding in my hand I am happy, smiling, hugging a gap-toothed brother wearing a mini-tuxedo complete with bow tie. What is happy anyway? Is my mother happy? Who is that woman with a perm anyway? She makes the bathroom smell like a crush of perfumed heaven; chemicals up in the air conspiring together and baby powder. I have no inclination of following in her footsteps. Feeding her children on hamburgers and mayonnaise as if they both were food groups.

All children are brats until they become the future leaders of the world. If my mother were a flower, she would not be a rose she would be a sunflower just because she burns that bright. When she is in the room, I would have to blink. Shut my eyes to really think. She makes me want to run away and hide and cry my eyes out when she tells me to shut up the preacher man can hear you. I have failed. Perfect timing. There is a bittersweet squalor in her voice. She is conserving so much energy in trying not to be genuine, sincere. Daddy is always lovely. Surely only love can cure me now. There is something physical, cerebral almost and it is not just the chemistry about being put under the spell of becoming fond of him (the lover) or loving him I simply wanted to become attached to his interests and his goals. He illumined the world, with his serious and funny ways and I wanted my world to be illuminated in the same way. I talk about the lover and my mum in the same voice. I use the same tone because I was left defeated in their wake. I trailed after them always masking my hurt and humiliation. It was not my journey to follow them, to follow their lead as I later learned with maturity and in ill health.

It is morning in Port Elizabeth. I still get the blues. At any time of the day, any time of the night. The fishing boats have gone out at sunrise. The ocean is miles away, out of sight behind factories, and the residential area. I cannot see it from my house even if I went and stood outside on the grass. I hear the cars on the road moving,

57

hooting, lights blinking. Kids in the park. There are truants smoking, girlfriend and boyfriend holding onto each other for life by the slide. Nothing in Port Elizabeth is as it is in Johannesburg. Life is quiet. I hardly see the neighbours. I have lived with that stillness for most of my life. I wanted to be a serious and funny and wise adult and the precocious child but learned that you could not do both. So I have my rituals all planned in from me. First, my coffee, then my work and then doubt levels the playing field. I can do this. My companions are my books. They are not in meetings the whole day. I am not twelve years old anymore. I have responsibilities. However, I cannot escape that mouth (mother's milk bitter and sweet) because it has become my mouth now on how I view the world.

Then raw and crass, shocking, explosive drama (all the usual stuff of a damaged and dysfunctional family) flies through the air. Plates too. Shut up the preacher man will hear you my mother will hiss. Doesn't she ever get a sense that this is familiar ground for her? How did I come this far with the language of a prostitute dying to belong? Some days I need poetry like I need life. In the olden days, poets truly were the masters of their own universe. My mother was like the Gestapo. She knew everything that was going to happen to me before I did. I did the acting in childhood part to please her. She helped me rehearse my lines. I brought home one year a trophy to please her. My sister is far away in her own ghost nation, late twenties, medium height, slender, eats organic (in the ghost nation of Johannesburg). Meanwhile I am growing older, early thirties, tall as a white reed. In some ways, I think I am dreaming when I think of any memories I have left of home. It is as if I'm awake and I'm dreaming at the same time.

It is as if it is another diary entry in just another black hole, void and journey on a page with strips of faultless blue lines. It is difficult for me to love again. I will have to examine whether I have put the pain I have experienced from experiences into a distillate all this time. The men that other women had committed their lives to, my lover and my mother all have one thing in common. They are con artists. They defraud hearts and hearts are delicate things. There is not much sense in messing around with them unless you want to destroy someone. If a parent does not invest everything, everything they have, own, and possess in the world in a child, in his or her own biological children what becomes of the child? Male destroyers turn the precocious child into a female destroyer. In addition, when that female enters their domain, she begins unknowingly to play by their rules because she has to keep up with them or otherwise she is forever lost to a cause. All the men will say merrily, your throne for their kingdom and when I was a child I laughed and I played at fairies and believed it was all fairy dust because I was raised that way (and because my father told me to). I was taught that men and women have very different roles to play in society. Equality did not mean anything to me as a child. In those days, it was different.

What I found in life and what I believed were two different things. God meant doing right by everyone even though they did you wrong. It meant going to church, devoting your life to raising your family in that environment, spiritual uplifting of the poor and the needy. What affairs of the heart will teach you is not so different. We are all the same. We want to be loved. We want to be ushered into this world with as much celebration and hoopla as possible. I was raised to believe in an ark. Nevertheless, even soon in that aftertime after important people in my life had moved on. When I left the most important adult relationship in my life, (the first boyfriend, and the first in a long steady line), I began to move away from things of the spirit world. In fact, to me the entire world was primed to be covered in a sense with a darker shield of magic and I knew that I unknowingly now I too had become a destroyer.

Writing with the glamour of Sylvia Plath, Anne Sexton and Jenny Zhang

By using my powers of observation as a child; that is how the English language, verse, the rhythm and internal rhyme of words came to me, came at me from the symmetry of my gut. Growing up the eldest of three children, my father drilled 'responsibility is key when it comes to your younger siblings' into the fabric of my mind. I always wrote. I had diaries in which I would bare the darkest secrets of my soul when I was a girl. I keep journals even now. I love the stream of consciousness writing that comes from journaling. I love putting staccato-like pencil to paper, watching the vast wilderness of your consciousness unfold within the demonstrative blossoming sight of your imagination. I do write full time and I am a workaholic. Everything is a process. Writers and poets by nature are sensitive and intuitive. I do not know if this happens with all writers from other countries but I do know this. African writers write in blood. It is in the ladders of their genes. If I said, 'I don't like to talk about my new work. It means I'm getting ahead of myself.' What would that mean; that I am arrogant, think highly of myself, that I am above other writers and poets? Humility continually cuts a writer's ego down to size. I am constantly thinking aloud about whatever I am working on and I have to make notes. I think if I told you what I was working on, I do not think you would completely believe me. My memoirs, another prose poetry book is in the works, I am constantly writing or working on ideas for short fiction. The medium of being published online has certainly afforded me a lot of opportunities (that I wouldn't have had otherwise) and for that I will eternally be grateful for generous, hardworking editors who work behind-the-scenes who have given me 'lucky' breakthroughs and for those who have published my work in print.

That is a very difficult question for me to answer. I am most comfortable with the genre of memoir when I am in that frame of mind. It is when I feel I have the most freedom to speak my mind, to write as I please with no one telling me what to do, wanting to change this or that. When it comes to writing poetry, haiku, prose poetry I am like a caged bird when I am in that frame of mind. When I am most inspired, I am also most lost. There am I, changing the structure of a sentence, taking a phrase out, self-editing, editing, editing. It is never going to be perfect but to me it has to be as close as I can get. In addition, if it is not perfect then I feel that I have failed somehow in a way.

I would like to try my hand at writing science fiction. 'Mr. Goop' inspired me. Ivor W. Hartmann's story that won the Baobab Prize a few years ago.

Above all read African writers, read everything you can lay your hands on but most of all be you. In the end, the only thing that matters is between you and your God, truth and beauty, love and mourning, nothing and everything, faith and light. The continent that has inspired so many generations before you; will inspire other poets and writers and will continue to inspire you and I have been there. I have had pieces of work that have been rejected, ripped apart by a 'glassy-eyed' editor, so will you. It will not be, is not the end of the world.

Corruption does not discriminate. No one is immune to it. Everyone is fair game whether you are connected to high ranking politician or a powerful family or working in local government. Miners' working under deplorable conditions is nothing new. Alan Paton wrote about that in, 'Cry the Beloved Country' and this engrossing book has now been around for decades. It is now part of school curriculums.

The mines in South Africa have been part of the fabric of the consciousness, the landscape of this country since the inner workings of apartheid were put into motion. Nothing has changed and yet it seems on the surface that everything has. You hear about these stories every day and you become so desensitised to it and at the end of the day you realise that there is nothing really that you can do constructively, except keep the faith that things will gradually move off by itself in the direction from the worst of conditions to the better.

Of course, my heart bleeds for them, those miners. They are only human. They have families, wives and children. However, that is not the first things people see when they open up a newspaper in the morning with their coffee. To them, the miners, employment is employment is employment (they see it as nothing else) and that is why education is so important. It should not be addressed or implemented as a 'just cause'.

The sensitive and emotionally mature amongst us will not shy away from issues of the day that has to be addressed, not just for the sake of addressing them. To change anything today is a revolutionary mission but it is one that begins with clarity of vision, equality, respect and recognition of communities at the grass roots level slipping into being. (I hope I have answered your question to the best of my ability. Please feel free to continue with this line of discussion. You are opening up the void of a black hole.)

No and I must say this with huge emphasis. Service delivery in the rural areas, the townships where unemployment is high, skills development is low, is non-existent and so far nothing is forthcoming from the government of the day except it seems empty promises when local government elections roll around. There is crime, criminal syndicates operating in the major cities. Clean, running tap water, sanitation, waste removal and electricity should be high on the priority list because it concerns the poorest of the poor; the majority of the population is living in squalor, slums, raising their children, families literally on bread and water. What kind of society treats its most vulnerable citizens in such an unjust way? Children are raising children. Sisters and brothers are playing the role of the absent parent in their younger siblings' lives and that is the travesty, the legacy of HIV/AIDS has left behind in its wake.

Xenophobia is a large-scale diabolical injustice in South Africa. It is pure evil what the human race is capable of doing physically, emotionally and mentally to one another. It is unnatural and disturbing to see this level of poverty, crime and death in the aftermath of the 'Rainbow Nation' and 'African Renaissance'. People are selfish, self-absorbed and self-indulgent but what they do not realise is that the world does not owe them anything. We are so consumed by money, cars, employment, visions of glory, wealth, and personal success. You have to make your own way in this world even though mountains like punishment and stage fright are staring you down, at every turn, every corner with snake eyes.

The world we are living in today is a world filled with madness, wide-open despair and it is like a fire tugging at your heartstrings, the pathways of nerves that connect to your consciousness; the effects, the black head of depression and mental illness are everywhere to see. Its existence can no longer be furiously hidden away from view and denied. On the outside, everything glitters but inside there is still urgency for bittersweet freedom and a living, breathing self-awareness, I feel, for this nation.

I did not deliberately set out to leave apartheid out or not write about it. In the end, it just happened that way. It was not a conscious decision. Only when I began this conversation with you, did I realise just how much of a role I played as a 'witness' to this/these heinous crime/s committed, in the name of the law of the land of this country, at the time when apartheid was what people were thinking was triumphing over the weak, the infirm, the destitute at its peak.

Apartheid deserves a book all on its own. One subject under the sun that I feel I will take on as I mature more and more as a writer. It will be challenging. There is so much rage, sorrow, a visceral disconnect between people who were the 'privileged minority' during apartheid and then there were the 'shamed minority' living stuck in the trenches of poverty and death. There are a lot of things, themes of the South Africa that I knew as a child that I left out of it (the poetry book *Africa Where Art Thou*), when I look back on the book in retrospect. Yes, you are right. So much more could have been said, perhaps I should have spoken about it, the life experience of a majority living in a case of perpetual state of feeling anxious, humiliated to the core, self-conscious and apartheid closed in on me, every facet, aspect and abstract of my childhood, adolescence and youth. Not just me but an entire country. On the one hand, it was flourishing and on the other it was a complete paradigm shift; in other words, infinite good on the one side versus resident evil. I did not want to state the negative, the negative, the negative repeatedly because it was omnipresent in every sphere, realm, empire, castle wall, ivory tower that apartheid was built on. If I had a book of hellish negatives (as a writer you can't work in that oppressive and claustrophobic realm, I mean, I can't deliver what I feel to be my very best work) how would people be drawn to it, was what I asked myself over and over again?

Thinking about it, I am glad that I did not pay any sort of 'homage' to apartheid in my first book. The market here (South Africa) is saturated with books on that subject. No one talks about Africa, the continent, the people, the inhabitants in a way that I feel I do in my first book a collection of stories *Winter in Johannesburg*. I am happy with the book but can any writer or poet really say that they are completely happy or that they feel it is finished-ish? You always want to go back and change something and there is always something you are not happy with in the end, but in a way, it is also liberating to feel that way.

Of the brutality of my illness, 'Iris' is left in the corner. Love me up. Fill the void. Nothing, nothing ever seems to.

Iris the poet.

I am a formidable workwoman, workhorse by nature and an experimenter of sorts. Isn't every poet? I am also deeply moved by art, I have a passion for work, I am attracted to the vital energy of love, death and consciousness, God and movements, observations, spirituality. I hope to speak about life in my poetry, about how it anchors me when I need to be, when my thoughts need to be reined in and anchored and how it frees me in another sense, another world. This world that I reach out to, speak about and come into contact with is the world that finds itself in communities. Here neighborhoods occur of parallel dimensions of the meditative union, of feeling the nature of a supreme being, of the whole of familial love, the drama, greatness of life in poetry and how it is acknowledged, the dream sequence of dream sequences in words. I celebrate the private self of the Outsider in verse, the loneliness the Outsider feels, the blank pressure, the threshold, and the inclinations.

Iris again.

I often feel outside of myself in crowds, sitting in the car in traffic or even when I am by myself with the still, small voice, that internal monologue as if I am having an out of body experience without my permission. However, I firmly believed that it came with the territory. Poets must suffer, must brave the storms of tragedy, must deal with the blows life deals them, and must learn to be, jive and jest. They must learn to amuse themselves on their own. Poets are roses wrapped (trapped) in glass vases. What do you do in an empty space except to expect the complex, paint it in diverse colours and patterns? How do you go about organising it into a meaningful whole? Look, even my scars from childhood, youth, the country, and the personal attack of city-life are pure and the waste of the elegant wasteland inside my head. Even though I have a constant craving to put away the sun in a rain cloud of rage.

Iris's writing flowering after sickness and a funeral.

The tall grass was like moving pictures amongst the glowing ochre. It is written on us, isn't it? I can feel the solitude in a leaf, when trees whisper to each other, in the afterglow of twilight, that warm and balmy haze speaks to me, all the summer in it. I have lost all of them now that she has passed on. There is a disconnection on the telephone with all of them. I have nothing to say to any of them.

My aunt is dust now or an angel, stimulus or an impulse, a thought or a living in a dream world and I have been left on my own to flower, to adventure into the greatness of the unknown, its brutal and aggressive nature. I know something of those tokens. I must remain vigilant of the occurrence of mania; the mass of contradictions that arises with euphoric highs that explodes into life behind my eyes. It hustles me swiftly from stillness to the multiplicity of madness. I did not say good-bye properly. I did not cry.

Iris (wishing that her sister would speak to her) and Gracie on the telephone.

'We need the money. I'm just asking because we need it.'
'I don't know what you want me to say.'
'Okay Gracie (but I am just trying to sum it up the best way I know how). Thank you for listening anyway.'
'Okay then. Bye.'
'Goodbye (why do you have to be so cruel).'

The measurement problem.

'Daddy, I told myself I wouldn't telephone her.'
'But you did.'
'I know but it was a mistake. Mummy's side of the family they are all toxic for me. The being of the stigma of all mental illness is toxic. I do not want to have anything to do with them and that is my final say. Say I will not telephone her again. Please, just say it daddy. Help me.'

Welcome to Iraq.

'You can work.'

'So you're saying I'm lazy.'

'Bipolar hasn't stopped other people.'

'Who are these 'other people'? You mean people who come from money, who were raised to be good citizens? What do (the bloody hell dammit I am not a child you are talking over) you mean exactly by those words?'

Adam's Wish for his daughter Iris.

'If you say you won't Iris then you won't. It is as simple as that. What more do you want me to say?'

'It's as if Gracie is saying bipolar is my self-inflicting wound. As if I asked for it, that it is my fault. Of course, I am not expecting her to take responsibility to live my life for me. People do not change. Materialism is important to her. Lip-gloss is her god. How can I have a conversation with someone that I have nothing in common with?'

Catching ghosts by putting bags over their heads.

In those days, nobody spoke of mental illness. It is not as if people are talking about it now. They are writing about it, the wreck of its torment, its oppressive gestures and perhaps the physicality of it but it is still spoken in a hush. It is driven with hands and clenched fists behind closed doors into a private realm. There are no shortcuts when it comes to dealing with ghosts. You have to face them high, head on and with your chin up.

The invisible interpretation of inventing Sylvia.

69

For all her life Gracie treated her sister is as if she was a walking-taking-productive-functioning-disease. She was a cold and disenchanted pale figure of heat and red dust, scaling the walls of the netherworld of photography under world and sky. She walked with her Nikon around her neck a fraudulent poser. If she was pretty or lovely, fair or beautiful she knew it. She would never be my silver lining. She would always let pensive little me burn in her shadow. I have so much more to live for. My mother's mood is patient. She waits for the perfect moment to despise you, to kill you with a look or to catch you off guard. I believe she is never truly unkind without a purpose in mind. Ah, there is Sylvia, at her most feverish, most high and elevated to her pure height of mother when all her children are present, therein lies her mysterious destruction that is immortalized by its authentic twists, narrow paths.

Aspects of Iris's Mind and Poetry.
I will forever hold images of men, the strange memories that I have of them, the things of men as close to my heart as I hold my breath. They have been the ones who have shaped me culturally and otherwise. If it had not been for them, their airs, dalliances into a cold and cruel world, their sometimes-unforgiving domination, their force of control, their hierarchy I would not have the peace of mind I have today and that I am committed to keeping at all costs. The weather report, the heat and the rain. That is all we ever seem to talk about. We have nothing to say to each other. Cat-eyed, blood-dripping women that I no longer stalk surround me; no longer wish to have anything to say to. Women who are aunts, daughters, cousins and that most obscene word to me, they are mothers with children

who are learning to talk, act, and respond to the world around them like their mothers. God help us all.

Dialogue between two women who are getting older.

'Is it hot out there?'
'Is it raining?'
'Are the lights out?'
'How are you?'
'What did you cook today? Is there a fire burning in the kitchen?'
'What's the weather like/the traffic like on the roads?'
'Did you deliver flowers today?'
'Can I talk to my mother, please?
'Just hold on one second. She is in front. What are you guys doing?'
'We're doing nothing. Nothing as usual.'
'I know you like to sleep late (its afternoon). Did I wake you?'

Iris and Neil.

Shall I write a poem and compare your face to the sun. First on the list of terrifying suspense– Neil held my hand tightly in his. Nostalgia is searching through an album where my funny face is completely unrecognizable. I saw the moon this evening and I was grounded and composed by the stars in the sky. In one afternoon, I was swallowed up whole by a hike. We climbed over rocks, our spirits renewed by the sense of adventure. We washed our hands after our picnic lunch in a cooling stream. Memories are made of this. I wish that you were here with me now. I want to show you this book I found at a second-hand bookstore that I have already reread four times. I wonder if you will feel grieved at the same places, I did at the decisions the hard and successful characters made.

Iris on Art.

Art mirrors life. Hellish art mirrors hellish life. The gifted (the most gifted at this time in history) youth and young at heart are fighting through the medium of art. Writing is art. Poetry is art. Art is art. To protect our legacy we must make history and end poverty. The higher powers, the authorities, government, authority figures must push through the segregation issue. We, Africa (our country), the world, we are all crying to be born again. Art can generate a sense and a sensibility of self-worth. With climate change and the wreck of the recession that has hit all of us like a freight train there is a sense of an ending but this also means that there is the familiarity and explicit recognition of a novel beginning. Exposing the self to the magic and the psychological-bent to art constantly, driving its core and the very force that is has as it plays a pivotal, empirical role in society just means that now it is necessary for us to move from consciousness to consciousness like a riverbed drowning in the ocean-sea.

Notes on loneliness. And when I go to sleep, it is there and when I wake up it is still there. A half-dream that slips away and all at once it is in reach. I can feel it, I cannot see it but I can sense it intuitively. I cannot explain why. I cannot explain this quantum leap.

Give it back to me whatever was stolen by pagans

Her soap, undergarments, silk stockings, strands of hair lay everywhere for-the-world-to-see. Her perfume, cooking-skills and incense fills my head. She is preparing a roast, mapping it out with delightfully-nutritious-perfection-in-the-kitchen. We will all sit down to eat. With-the-family-life we've-been-storing-it-up. We are all starving with hunger. Pouring-the-stealing beauty-of-the-kitchen-table-and-the-lust-for-the-feast-in-front-of-us-into-all. Her eye is a map, her hands smell like jasmine, her hair like gossamer and she is his dream come true. Her laughter is a custard apple, a cabbage rose, never-ending. We drink tea for hours confiding in each other insanely hypomanic as we discuss men and the objects of her affection, her children, and her lover.

Bellies full of a pretty food chain, a location for a nurturing position, prep, even grief we tell each other comes with gifts (endurance and forgiveness, a reason to validate, to forget, have an opinion whether it be relevant or irrelevant), future leaders leaning towards being proactive. Even in a war, in Nazi Germany there are whores of Babylon, stockings, a Hitler with a moustache, a world where Mussolini an ally and propaganda, where all the dead can't be remembered, names forgotten everyone but once there was a pianist according to Polanski.

My head is lost in films, the opposite of the dark, a woman reading in a library, our South Africa, the Group Areas Act, my violent home, the brutality of man against man in my country. Yellow stars once upon a time marked a Jew's coat, their lovers and their spirits, scorched them, and burned their intellect, their talent, mocking seduction and betrayal, mocking a syndrome. Listen. Listen as it settles like violence, the sea. The mocking sea. One day it will either say remember me, like Ingrid Jonker's (my superior older sister) black butterflies inside her head or wash away your sins. I wonder about her contemporaries, her lovers, her Brink, her Andre. The sea is mocking me. This great event that lies before me dying and living, giving away and receiving, nurturing schools, shark teeth, and a feast of eyes. In front of the poet lies the landscape, the hill, the valley, the mountain, and the playing fields. The intelligent mind is appalled by the needle and the knife.

There is a heavy sensation at play, a freeze and an arrangement of sorts that pales in comparison to anything else that life seems to offer, an appealing curation. It chills me to the bone that I am not wearing that white wedding lace, that ring and there is gossamer fairy thread in the clouds above and a silver lining in every one. I am a shell. Shadows lurk under the bed, in the closet. He does not turn back. I am falling (an antique). I am an old soul that no one can understand, fathom, explain love, passion, having a spouse and companion too. She is old before her time. They all say that whoever they, they might be.

The community, estranged and immediate family, the stigma, the neighbours. It is not normal not to have a child, children, drive a car (my mother is superior to me in every way but I know that a long time ago over a decade this was not the case). It is not normal to live in the reality that I live in with recovery after recovery after suicidal illness and how disability has become familiar to me. First in my father's life and now in mine. I am left to dream. I am left to dream of a Saviour who will rescue me on this ghost planet. Elizabeth Wurtzel's Prozac Nation. I find sanctuary, peace of mind reading in a sofa. I find myself amongst my books and writing grants. South Africa can learn from Germany.

South Africa can learn from Sarajevo. South Africa can learn from genocide, the holocaust, and the rest of the African continent. Her beautiful people, their diamond smiles, creamy-velvet skin and their bravery, their bold survival, their sensuality, how they have managed being silenced about slavery, their footsteps in the dark, the beating of the drums, watermelons and mangoes, donkeys and carts. The enemy is the thief, the man and the woman, the German who causes heartache, what was really behind the Nazi vision? Hitler and his moustache? Was it an altered state of mind and separation anxiety? The rat's spine is broken. It is a bleeding mass on the concrete. The dog has got to it first before the glued mousetrap. People who are hungry enough eat rats, squirrels too. Rats can be people too. If children are lucky enough they only learn that later in life after layers and layers of experience.

Germany was like South Africa a time out of place for some time, walls were built brick by brick literally and figuratively amongst the different race groups. It is still not forgotten. The people here have a long memory. The haves and the have-nots in a time not of their own making, an identity theory that is misplaced yet idolised at the same time, represented as the highest ideal and idea to live for and we believe that there is no revolution, no personal space for it, it is evaporated like smoke. Where do the moths go when daylight comes if they are so attracted to the light? Do they come and go as an angel comes and goes.

It leaves a white feather as a reminder to tell us, 'I have been here watching over you, watching over your household, your garden, your memories of the people in your life who have passed on to the hereafter. I see you in the kitchen preparing meals for your family. I see your love, affection and adoration for the little ones, for the big ones, for the giants and the greats that have lived and struggled, who were valiant. I see you when you are working, when you are fighting with something deep within yourself, your hurt, your ego and how you pray and meditate for yourself and for the young people around you, for their intellect.' So angels come and angels go like sadness and suffering and ritual and ceremony, thanksgiving and pilgrimages and the theory of identity in a time that is not fluent but sometimes fluent in energy and variety. In South Africa, the Jews are a minority group like those of us who wear white masks and go by the name of Coconut.

I have been shamed, have felt ashamed, humiliated by the colour of my skin, the sound of my posh voice that bounced off walls sounding like a sonnet, British-English from Speech and Drama lessons, sounding so articulate for a mixed race young girl (how I remember how other girls made me cry in the school bathroom during lunch break until I could no longer hold my breath, called me 'Alice why do you talk that way funny little thing' as I walked past them in the hallways, and in the street when I walked home after school. They called me other names, bullied me senseless until I became a mute like Princess Diana and Maya Angelou when they were children, lost myself, lost my voice only to find it on a stage, in the spotlight, in plays, rehearsals, reciting, reciting, learning lines parrot-fashion, garnered lead and supporting roles at the Opera House in Port Elizabeth and a house play, a school play).

I only found my voice when I discovered other poets and poetry. Home was not so great. Now I know all Southern Africans have accents. The margin is there in Southern Africa between the fortunate, brave, and those who have no skills and are unemployed. Black faces, chocolate, white faces, vanilla and those of mixed

76

heritage, Cape Malay, Muslim, coloured, Rastafarian. We're all living together and not together in a scorched climate, a summer and a winter, rain pouring down which some of us receive with joy as we curl up with wine, olives and cheese and pasta and others, the invisible others whose homes are flooded, whose little food is washed away, wasted away. It is still the same for them. Has always been for years, the Rainbow Nation and the African Renaissance has come and gone but they come to me in dreams. I see them in front of me. I feel what they feel. I see what they see and it is not pretty, dignified or nice in any way. Their suffering tears into me. I flinch.

In addition, it is always their hunger that is never diminished, that fact is not wasted on me. Their children do their homework by candlelight or not at all. What do they eat? Is it any wonder that they do not grow normally, tall, dark and handsome, and why is it only the younger children that smile and play. Toys are not enough for their world. They need to eat, bread and milk and sandwiches (no eggs and bacon for the poor, fried mushrooms that taste as slimy as snails are for the rich, as is shellfish). Where is the birthday cake with balloons the colours of crayons? And every day they remember when it rained? How do they sleep, at school?

How do they keep their wide eyes open with their long lashes when there is a gust of wind through a broken window, when the rain is also an element on the Periodic Table, when there is no roof over their heads in the classroom, when there is a protest march in the community over service delivery? Why do the rich get richer in South Africa and the poor get poorer in South Africa on a daily basis? Children need people, adults to believe in them, have faith in them. All I see now on television, in the newspaper before I turn to read the comics is violence and guns like the night there were police and plainclothes detectives in our house confronting my brother. It

77

was almost as if it was Warsaw, Poland and we were playing dress-up. As if we all were in futuristic costume. But I promised to look after him and they brought him back from the police station that night because he had promised to make no more trouble. No more trouble for my father who he had beaten up.

My father in his threadbare white vest, (no mistaking a potbelly) stained thick with blood, and sweat wearing shorts showing his skinny legs. He had smashed the windows with a brick scaring us all half-to-death like a tik-addict looking for a fix, an upper or a downer. Then he broke down, cried like a baby. The vulnerable part inside of him was shattered. I was shattered. They took him away but brought him back again. Jews. Jews. Jews. Yes, I believed in the inherent goodness of people (but then a genocide took place in Africa in front of the world's eyes documented in the film Hotel Rwanda). Just like a serving dish of sky, the blades of Whitman's grass, autumn leaves, trees almost-conjured-up-out-of-the-ground, youth-not-yet-cuckoo-in-the-bird's-nests-of-their-brains you will never forget the films you see that changes you for life. The films of war-torn Germany, genocide and the fact that there is not a film or a documentary about the forced removals.

Oh, there are museums but do they talk about the memory of that time's frustration, 'the struggle', political activists that were recruited like my father when he was just seventeen years old along with his best friend and his brother. George Botha. Arthur Nortje. Dennis Brutus. Richard Rive. I want them to live forever like my 'wild Sargasso' sea. The District Six Museum, The South End Museum, The Red Location Museum, The George Botha Memorial Lecture by storyteller and Professor Cornelius Thomas of Rhodes University in Grahamstown who studied at Notre Dame University in North America.

The world does not promise everyone a rose garden, that you will be born with a silver spoon in your mouth, that the world will be your oyster. I think of Virginia Woolf 'Her black butterflies' and that fateful day of how if I had been there, a witness I would have said to her, 'Turn back. Turn back because you are surely going to hell. You cannot take your own life. It is not your time.' However, I was not there. I am here now in this South Africa surrounded by faces of every hue, hair of every texture. Violence does not seem to fade into the night, the moonlight, gunshots ring out, and there are ganglands even as I write this.

Even as I speak to my father in the morning over mugs of lukewarm coffee filled with powdered cream, no sugar because he is a diabetic as he rests, does his exercises-and-recovers-from-them but are we as far away from the 'war zone' on the streets of Gelvandale, Port Elizabeth as we think we are? The sexual, physical, and domestic violence? The prostitutes in their flats in Central with their stiletto heels, boots, their lipstick, wigs, cheap perfume, powders and ointments to make their partner's 'experience' more pleasurable.

And I remember the face of this girl. Her name long forgotten but not her dark mane. Jewess. Moreover, I think of Otto and his daughter's diary.

The cat lady standing in front of the door of flames

I have often spoken about death. Sometimes it comes like a loud shout, a big bang deliberately but sometimes it is strangely quiet as if there is a royalty to its element. And then there is the earth that we fold the body physically into, throw dust on it and pay our respects or the ash that we hold in our hands. And then afterwards when the family gathers to eat, to sup together, to break bread there are a lot of things I assume they surrender, that they let go of or don't. Head under water is the only place I can let go of all of these things. There is no echo, nothing to distract me here, evaporate me like smoke. And it is the only place where I find God. It is not rain pouring down, wires of serotonin, dopamine, electrolytes growing from my head, nightmares that come to me in the middle of the night that worries me so, and illness.

Its skin was red, orange and green, tasted like butter. A mango is delicious from the first time you taste it and I tasted my first proper mango in Swaziland (all that goodness came with its warmth, that sweetness on my breath, juice on my clothes, sticky fingers but shadows must meet somewhere and all I wanted to see was London). I remember the mangoes you kept for me until I came home from school (you would put it in the fridge until it was cool, the orange strings of flesh). We would have avocado on toast, or French toast with fresh coriander leaves fried in creamy butter or hotdogs and chips as only you could make them where Swaziland was my home for a year. You died before your time, my second mother. Your hands pale, hair dark and as you became more ill with the more weight you lost but you were still beautiful to me. Leaves shake and rot in autumn, spin around, and around. You were my bright star amongst all souls. I miss epic you every day. There is a loss that comes with breathing. However, the stranger in the ghost house has no voice. He does not speak of self-help, a shelf life. A double life, red dust, dead parakeets, sweat running down his wife's back, the madness and despair of Liberace. Something is unanchored yet still beautifully functions, is productive. It is called family and the awareness of coming home, a flag was planted here in the South's wilderness where a genocide took place, there is whisky in a glass, an afternoon cocktail. Books that are a sanctuary. An Eric Clapton record is playing. The red dust of this county does not speak of self-help. There is a suicide. A death in a river. In addition, the police have come. This is August: Osage County.

The police come in the middle of the night. Like the detectives in plainclothes that came to my house in the middle of the night when my brother took a knife and stabbed my father. Nothing romantic about it. About the onslaught of death, of it catching up to you like a thief in the night, a cat burglar, a cat drowning in a bag with her kittens, that is how I felt as if I was a drowning visitor. I saw guns that night I led a double life. I pretended I did not see or hear anything and inside I was numb. When I saw my father's blood it had an oppressive quality to it like everything in my life so far. The drugs refused to work. So I took more and more of them, slept all day and all night.

The double life of the romantic jasmine. It lives, it dies, it lives, and it dies like people. I can talk and talk and no one will be listening to my conversations, eavesdropping. Down the winter road, I came across men who stare at goats. Men who were good dancers or American soldiers who took German lovers during the war. Men who were good actors, some were heavy drinkers in my mind, and

81

philanthropists. The knife was sharp. It struck air repeatedly and again. Then it was anchored in skin. I did not scream. I was a Scout's knot. I ran in my floppy sandals to the neighbour's house as fast as my feet could carry me. Outside the air felt cool as rain. How I wished it had rained? But there was no rain that night and they called the police.

There is no romance in death. Hair and flesh coming loose. Still daddy was left standing, unafraid. My brother was prancing around all of us, smirking, smiling with cunning deceit, high he was having his cake and eating it too. Pinned daddy to the bed with his arms like shark teeth. My mother had run away in the dark. I was left with notes of grief, a stem and a route to follow. A flowering-bleeding heart making waves, beating fast. It was Christmas. However, there were no presents only a winter road to follow.

To hell with it if I do not ever fall in love. It is a case of much ado about nothing. I have lost my mind and recuperated in hospitals. Once again, become anchored to reality in recovery. I do not have a brother and I do not have a sister. I do not have a mother and I do not have a father. They live their own lives, so they amuse themselves, selfish people everyone. While I am kept sheltered in Pandora's Box. It is a box filled with romantic villagers of my own making. What a comfort they are to me. I am an orphan on Okri's famished road. I am Nabokov's and Kubrick's Lolita. Soon I will be forgotten like breath. The moveable a feast of sex, romance and death. Damaged, damaged, damaged but I must not speak of it. It will be the death of me and I must live without the disease, the stain of trauma a while longer, sit on my throne, collect bones like arrows that fall from the sky. Curiosity has killed me. Men have killed me extraordinarily. But I have nine extraordinary lives and am left smiling like the Cheshire cat.

This is the brother who I am supposed to love. I do not admire him anymore. I feel nothing for him when I remember that night from hell. House of hunger. House of hell, of madness and despair. If he had a gun, we all would be dead. I cut up the onion, seduced by its layers. And I cry for what has been lost, gems every one. There are diamonds in my eyes and I blink them back. My youth, my youth, my youth and there is no ring. No ring on my finger, all those chronic wasted years. Now he is Lucifer manning the gate to the wards of hell. My beautiful, darling boy what has become of you?

The secrets that we keep are committed to memory. They're lessons in the needs of people around us, a lesson in obedience, sometimes even wisdom. And it takes bold work for us to realise that the future is bright when sometimes we are challenged, when we have to mine glory. And make a ceremony out of it. There are profound ingredients that goes into making a spaghetti bolognaise. Family is of course the first priority. Next the butcher, mint from the garden and limes for the cocktails. Footsteps on the stairs and laughter scribbling in the air.

Perhaps avocadoes were the first fruits (food for thought) in the Garden of Eden even before Eve was made from Adam's rib via the maturation of a human soul and a vortex in flux.

Sun and moon. They are miracle angelic beginners every one each day. Daughters nicknamed so for jasmine and yesterday, today and tomorrow. Then as if woken up from a dream, the day begins.

Head under water. Silently pushing off from the wall of the swimming pool doing lap after lap. Here is where I find my sanctuary, my second home and solace from the world outside. I am not like the other girls. They're all younger, thinner, and confident even though they're still flat-chested and flirtatious from where I am standing. Head under water again. I'm praying it won't be the house from hell again tonight. I'm watching films, reading books, wiping my father's bum (there are no secrets between us). We talk about our past lives, our nine lives, love and the measure of it, how the devil made work for idle hands during apartheid, during the promulgation of the Group Areas Act, the Nazi war lords, Hotel Rwanda. We talk about the women in his life, past and present, the first woman he ever loved and lost and the measure of it. I become distracted. He becomes distracted and I get up to make cups of coffee, lukewarm coffee. We discuss Valkenburg (the mental institution in Cape Town where he resided for a few months).

The first social worker he ever met. This is all for the book I am writing. Walking in his footsteps. Night after night, I make a casserole and the two of us sit down to eat at the kitchen table. He walks, he shuffles, he walks, and he shuffles. Sometimes he sits outside with Misty, the dog in the sun. He is forgetful, he stammers, he has a short attention span but then again I guess memory loss comes with age. Last night he wet the bed. There are people who would make a mockery of this situation but when you're knee deep in it with someone that you love, intimacy is nothing, acknowledging that he is becoming older is everything. I've become an old woman overnight. Suddenly I have grey hair, the wisdom of a lake, a slight tremor in my hands, I suffer from anxiety, and I can't sleep at night. He calls for me in the middle of the night. He needs me and so this teaches me that I am not cruel like the others (other members of the family). I am a woman now. Something has replaced the darkness in my life. I have discovered the stem of meditation.

Its face, its route, my life's journey in this crowded house and tears. My mother does the laundry. Not such a terrible woman after all. If only all women could be like her. Tough. Made of holy guts, an insatiable instinct, almost a clairvoyant instinct. She lives like a nun and eats like one these days. She eats like a bird making soup, after soup after soup that only the three of us eat. As an adult, I have fallen in love with the terrific goodness of barley and the healthy protein of lentils. Split peas reminds me of eating a home cooked meal in the afternoon's at my paternal grandmother's house in the afternoons. My paternal grandmother's hands were beautiful. Wizened because she suffered from arthritis, dark brown. Warm with the texture of the sun and freckled. She was my moon, my moonlight and elegant. She offered us bowls of soup with home baked bread that tasted more nourishing and filling than the shop bought expensive kind. My mother promises us all a long life if we drink blends of herbs.

Dried rosemary, tinctures, tonics, homemade green smoothies with parsley, spinach from our vegetable patch and coconut milk. Head under water I reflect, I meditate, I breathe easy. I swim with the fishes, schools of them in this swimming pool. It lights a candle in my heart when I swallow water. My brother makes stews with his home-grown carrots and corn. All I can make is spaghetti. Frieda's spaghetti. It is so cold now. The world feels so cold. It feels as if Iraq has descended into my thoughts again. Sarajevo. Rwanda and the children of northern Uganda. I am a young woman on the verge of a nervous breakdown. I must be strong to carry on, remain brave, act bold. Sometimes I can hear Tchaikovsky. My father has taken to his bed. He has depression again (the-William-Styron-kind). I wonder if John Updike ever suffered from depression. I know Hemingway certainly did. What about J.M. Coetzee, Radclyffe Hall, Vladimir Nabokov, Kubrick, Tennessee Williams? And the filmmakers, writers, the poets who were heavy drinkers?

But I leave that in God's hands for his commentary, all those signals. I'm old before my time. I'm an old soul. Complicated, an empty vessel, envious of beauty like any woman, of youth, of the girl, of children in childhood. My babies are my books.

And sometimes I feel dead inside (not numb or cold). As if I have a subconscious mind that's crossed over. As if I am lame, pathetic, stupid and have one blue eye. Blue as the sky on a wild Saturday and the other green. As green as a mocking sea, mocking school of fishes carrying on, surfing along, swimming by on their own survival skills with their world occurring in an awful dead blue silence.

With the fingers of the sky so far away from them.

The page frees me in a sense, in a way I cannot describe. I write and that is my life. I am not a mother and a wife, not a lover, but a poet, and I feel that is also just a part of my life. Sometimes the two meet and sometimes they do not. Sphere upon sphere upon another sphere. Poetry is a god to me. When I write I am a woman on her own. Reality is out of the picture and it does not seem to count for anything really. It is never enough for me. I stand and watch the busyness of life, observing nature and most of all human nature and I slowly empty out. It is a useful exercise kind of like transcendental meditation. I know nothing about it. It is just something I read as a girl in a book long ago when I was at school and at the time, it was just too much for me to handle. The thought of going out of myself made me go numb and cold. It gave me the shivers. If I was alone I would go mad with grief and rage and I would be that girl again.

When I enter the body of poetry a sense of fulfilment and satisfaction washes over me. There are explosions of tiny waves behind my eyes. My soul has made it thus far. I have to end the poverty in my mind but I find a cold comfort in the not knowing of things. If depression happened in nature, what would we call it then? Would it be organic in origin? In a marriage when it ends whom is to blame for its demise. Who is the culprit? On the approaching betrayal in any relationship, I have this to say. Lock down your heart dear and look away. It means that there may be something incomplete in the moving against the current of love. It means to love and die simultaneously. I think there is a theory behind light. When my body feels full of that stuff, the light, and the hidden energies in my aura, I feel as if I have free tickets to the centre of winter.

Printed in the United States
By Bookmasters